The World in a Nutshell

Iran

in a nutshell

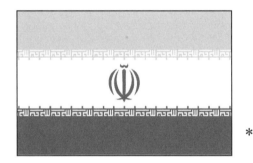

*

Enisen Publishing

Iran in a Nutshell

*FLAG

Before 1979, Iran's flag had three horizontal bands. The green band on top represented Islam, white in the middle represented peace and the bottom red band meant courage. A lion holding a sword standing in front of the rising sun adorned the center.

After the 1979 Islamic Revolution, the lion emblem was replaced by a stylized representation of the word **Allah** (God) [see below]. The five lines making up the word are in the shape of a tulip, the symbol for martyrdom, and they also stand for the five principles of Islam. Other sources describe the emblem as a sword, denoting strength, encircled by a globe, representing the worldwide growth of the Muslim faith.

Between the top and bottom bands are two rows with the words "Allahu Akbar" ("God is Great") written in Arabic and repeated 11 times on each line. The numbers 11 and 22 (the total number of repetitions of the phrase) signify the date of the Islamic Revolution which took place on the 22nd day of the 11th month according to the Iranian calendar.

Emblem   "Allah" (Arabic)

***

Special thanks to Avo Tavitian who made this and all Nutshell Notes books possible.

Note: This book uses the initials B.C. ("before Christ") and A.D. ("Anno Domini" or "in the year of our Lord") rather than B.C.E. ("Before the Common Era") and C.E. ("in the Common Era") for dating purposes since the writer and editors felt these terms were more familiar to Nutshell Notes readers.

We understand that future activities may modify or shed new light on some of the data in this book. For that reason, Nutshell Notes, LLC and Enisen Publishing invite readers to visit our website www.enisen.com to learn about the latest developments concerning Iran.

Iran in a Nutshell
First edition – March 2006
First published – March 2006

Enisen Publishing
2118 Wilshire Boulevard, #351
Santa Monica, CA 90403-5784
(866) ENISENP 866 364-7367
http://www.enisen.com
publishing@enisen.com

Text	Amanda Roraback
Maps	Katie Gerber
Editors	Medgar Boston, Angela Lord and John Palmer
Editor-in-Chief	Dorothy A. Roraback

ISBN 978-0-9763070-1-3
Printed in the United States of America

TABLE OF CONTENTS

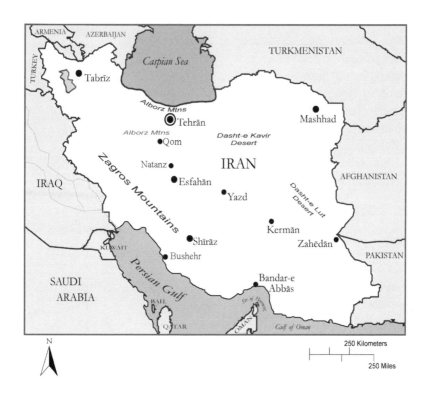

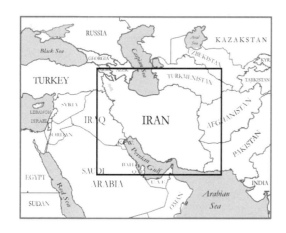

FACTS AND FIGURES*

Country Name: Islamic Republic of Iran
Known as Persia until 1935 then called Iran
Became Islamic Republic of Iran in 1979

Government Type: Theocratic republic (government ruled by religious authority)

Chief of State: Supreme Leader Ayatollah Ali Hoseini-**Khamenei**
(since June 1989, appointed for life)

Head of Government: President Mahmud **Ahmadinejad**
(since Aug. 2003, next elections to be held in 2009)

Capital City: Tehran

Independence: October 3, 1932 League of Nations mandate under
British administration.

Population: 68,017,860 (July 2005 est.)
About 70% of Iran's population is under the age of 30.

Ethnic Groups: Persian 51%, Azeri 24%, Gilaki and Mazandarani 8%,
Kurd 7%, Arab 3%, Lur 2%, Baloch 2%, Turkmen 2%,
other 1%

Religion: Shi'a Muslim 89%, Sunni Muslim 9%, Others 2%
(Zoroastrianism, Jewish, Christian, Bahai)

Languages: Persian and Persian dialects 58%, Turkic and Turkic
dialects 26%, Kurdish 9%, Luri 2%, Balochi 1%, Arabic
1%, Turkish 1%, other 2%

Literacy: total population: 79.4% (male: 85.6% female: 73%)

Currency: Iranian rial

Export partners: Japan 18.4%, China 9.7%, Italy 6%, S. Africa 5.8%, S. Korea
5.4%, Taiwan 4.6%, Turkey 4.4%, Netherlands 4% (2004)
(1987 U.S. imposed trade embargo still in effect).

Import partners: Germany 12.8%, France 8.3%, Italy 7.7%, China 7.2%,
UAE 7.2%, South Korea 6.1%, Russia 5.4% (2004)

Exports: Petroleum 80%, chemical and petrochemical products,
fruits and nuts, carpets

Oil production: 3.979 million barrels of oil (bbl) per day
(2nd largest producer among member nations of OPEC)

GDP per capita: $8,100 (2005 est.) (Income decreased by 30% from1980- 2000)

Size: 0.64 million square miles, slightly larger than Alaska

*Figures taken primarily from the CIA World Factbook 2005 - Iran

BACKGROUND

ELAMITES (2700 B.C. – 559 B.C.)

The first tribes who settled within the present borders of Iran after the ice age lived in scattered and secluded villages and towns isolated between large mountain ranges and vast deserts. They were first unified in the mid-3rd millennium B.C. by the Elamites[1] who established their capital in Susa[2] in southwest Iran (present-day Khuzestan province).

To the west of the Elamite kingdom in Mesopotamia[3] (present-day Iraq) lived the Sumerians[4] and Akkadians with whom the Elamites alternately traded and fought. When the Elamites and their neighbors were at peace, they exchanged cultural practices and traded goods (the Elamites were renowned for their metalwork). When at war, they seized and sacked each others' cities.

In the 7th century B.C., the Elamites were finally defeated when the highly militaristic **Assyrians** (who had taken over Mesopotamia around 1200 B.C.[5]) devastated Susa in retaliation for the Elamites attacks on the Mesopotamians through the preceding centuries.

ARYANS[6]

Throughout the 2nd millennium B.C., while the Elamites were trying to defend their land from the Sumerians, the Akkadians and the Assyrians, a wave of Indo-European Aryans arrived from Central Asia.

The fair complexioned, nomadic Aryans migrated from their homeland between the Black and Caspian Seas in search of greener pastures for their horses, warmer weather and a more peaceful lifestyle. Some went west to Europe to eventually become the ancestors of the Greeks, Romans, Celts and Teutons. Another group went to India[7] through Afghanistan, and a third to Iran, settling in Elam. According to the ancient Greek historian, **Herodotus**, the Indo-European groups who landed in present-day Iran fell into two groups, the **Medes**, who settled in the northwestern parts of Iran bordering Assyrian territories, and the **Persians** or Parsa who settled in the southwest

---

[1] In the Hebrew bible, the Elamites are described as the offspring of Elam, the eldest son of Shem and grandson of Noah (who survived the great flood by building an ark).

[2] They are sometimes called Susanians.

[3] "Mesopotamia" (meaning "between the rivers" in Greek) lies between the Tigris and Euphrates rivers in present-day Iraq. It is believed that the Garden of Eden, the abode of Adam and Eve, was in Mesopotamia.

[4] The Sumerians were the first to develop writing by using wedge-like symbols called *cuneiform* and the number system based on 60 units (today used to tell time). The Epics of Gilgamesh, which included the first references to the story of the great flood, were also written by the Sumerians.

[5] The Assyrian Empire stretched from Armenia to present-day Syria. In order to prevent revolts in the occupied areas, the Assyrians forced conquered peoples to migrate to other areas in the empire. They ruled in northern Mesopotamia from 1200-612 B.C..

[6] The name "Iran" derives from the word "Aryan" (meaning "noble" or "Lord" in Sanskrit).

[7] The "Indo-Aryans" settled in the Harappan civilization of the Indus valley. Indo-Aryan society was divided into four classes based on skin color introducing the caste system that still exists in India.

in what is now the **Fars** province.[8]

MEDES (900 B.C. – 550 B.C.)

Both the Medes and the Persians established capitals and founded cities in the region, but it was the Medes[9] who exacted tribute from their Persian kinsmen and dominated the ancient Iranian plateau for centuries.

Around 800 B.C., the Medes began to expand their empire into Mesopotamia. Under their greatest ruler, **Cyaxares**, the Medes overthrew the Assyrians with the help of the Babylonians and expanded their empire west to the eastern portion of Anatolia (present-day Turkey). The capture of the Assyrian capital of Ninevah in 612 B.C. marked the end of the 600 year- old Assyrian Empire. Assyria was subsequently divided amongst the Babylonians, the Medes and the Egyptians.

PERSIANS/ACHAEMENIDS (550 B.C. – 330 B.C.)

While the Medes were battling with the Assyrians,[10] their Persian vassals were developing into a force of their own. A few years after the fall of Nineveh, **Cyrus II**, the king of a Persian kingdom called **Ansan**, formed a coalition of tribes and led them in battle against Cyaxares's son **Astyages**, successor to the Median throne, . By 550 B.C. the Persians had won a decisive victory and **Cyrus** ("**the Great**") became the new ruler of the Persian and Median **Achaemenid** Empire[11] (named after the renowned warrior, **Achaemenes** who was an ancestor of Cyrus's).

With the Persians and Medes united, Cyrus (580-529 B.C.) and his army continued to expand the Empire. After defeating the Lydians[12] in 546 B.C., the Persians swiftly conquered **Babylon**, (539 B.C.) which had become the most powerful state in the ancient world after the fall of the Assyrian empire.

Once in Babylon, Cyrus liberated prisoners who, according to Babylonian custom, had been forced to relocate from their conquered lands. Among them were the Hebrews from Judah who had been living in captivity in Babylon since Babylonian **King Nebuchadnezzar** occupied Jerusalem in 597 B.C..[13] Accounts of Cyrus's benevolence and the Hebrews' return to their homeland were later documented in the Torah (biblical Old Testament), the Hebrew holy book. (See Chronicles II 36:22023 and Ezra 1:1-4.)

The flattering accounts of Cyrus in the Bible corresponded with his historical reputation as a tolerant and generous leader. Cyrus preserved indigenous governmental institutions, respected local customs and religions and even

---

[8] The Persians called the area Parsa. The word Fars (as in "Farsi," the Persian language) derives from Pars.

[9] The term "Mede" remained in European usage as a synonym for "Persian" for millennia.

[10] To the Persians, the Median Empire, which bordered the Assyrian Empire, acted as an ideal buffer state between the Assyrians and the Persian territory. The Persian isolation allowed them to develop into a power of their own.

[11] Although they were the victors, the Persians considered the Medes equals and allowed prominent Medes to retain important positions.

[12] The Lydians lived in the western part of present-day Turkey.

[13] For more on the Hebrews and the Babylonian Captivity see Roraback's, Israel-Palestine in a Nutshell.

penned the first known **Charter of Human Rights**.[14]

As the Persians swept through the region, they introduced Persian art, literature, architecture and their newly adopted monotheistic religion, **Zoroastrianism,**[15] to the region.

By the time Cyrus the Great died in battle in 530 B.C. he had created the greatest empire the world had known at that time. His son and successor, **Cambyses II** (530-522 B.C.) was determined to expand the empire even further to Egypt through a number of campaigns that ended in his death and rebellion at home.

After a brief civil war over succession, a general and a distant cousin of Cambyses II called Darius I was crowned the new Persian king.

Under the command of **Darius I** (later known as **Darius the Great**), the empire was divided into a number of *satrapies* (relatively autonomous provinces ruled by a Satrap or Governor who made annual payments to the central government at **Persepolis**.)[16] The *satrapies* were connected to each other by an elaborate infrastructure of roads, and communication between the regions was made possible by an ancient version of the Pony Express messenger system linked by more than 100 stations[17] To facilitate trade, Darius introduced a coinage system (a gold coin called a "Darik" was minted), established an elaborate banking system, standardized weights and measures and constructed a canal connecting the Red Sea to the Nile River which flowed to the Mediterranean Sea.

At the height of Darius's rule, the empire had expanded from India to Egypt and north to the Bosporus (separating present-day Turkey and Greece). But Darius's ambition to expand the empire to Europe was thwarted by two decades of battles against the Greek city-states.[18]

The **Greco-Persian wars** were triggered by a rebellion in 498 B.C. by the Ionian Greeks who had been living under Persian rule on the western coast of Asia Minor. When the Persians tried to crush the rebellion by burning their center, Sardis, the Ionian Greeks asked for help from other Greek city-states, including Athens and Sparta.

The Persians were defeated at the **Battle of Marathon** by the vastly outnumbered Greek forces, destroying the myth of Persian invincibility.[19]

---

[14] For a full transcript of the Charter, please visit www.enisen.com.

[15] It has been theorized that Cyrus liberated the Hebrews and helped them rebuild their temple in Israel because he saw their god, Yahweh, as a "good" god and ally of Ahura Mazda, the Zoroastrian god.

[16] The city of Persepolis (from the word "Pars" and "polis" meaning city) is in the present Fars province of Iran.

[17] The ancient historian, Herodotus, praised the Persian "postal" system by claiming "neither rain, nor snow, nor heat nor gloom of night keeps these couriers from the swift completion of their appointed rounds." Centuries later (1913) the quotation was inscribed on the façade of the New York City General Post Office building and became the motto for the U.S. Postal Service.

[18] At the time, Greece was divided into more than 1000 small city-states with Athens and Sparta being the most prominent.

Ten years later, Darius's son, **Xerxes**, attempted, once again, to defeat the Greeks. By that time, though, the Greeks had united into the **Hellenic League** (481 B.C.)[20] and put up a more determined fight. After a few battles (during which the Persians set fire to Athens), **Xerxes's** fleet was defeated (479 B.C.) ending Persian domination in the area.[21]

Once the Persian threat was eliminated, though, the Greek city-states began to fight among themselves in the Peloponnesian War. Twenty seven years of conflict between Athens and Sparta and their allies left the Greek city-states too weak to resist the rise of Philip of Macedonia whose kingdom was just north of Greece.

King Philip, a man of great ambition, saved his kingdom from imminent disintegration, built the Macedonian military into an invincible force and set out to conquer the world through war and diplomacy. Philip created alliances by marrying women from six different kingdoms, including Olympias from Epirus who bore him a son, named **Alexander III**.

With his formidable army, Philip seized the kingdoms of Thessaly and Thrace north of Macedonia by 352 B.C. and in 338 B.C. defeated an alliance of Greek states which included Thebes, Athens, Sparta and others. After adopting the new title of "Commander of the Greeks," Philip prepared to invade Greece's longtime enemy, Persia. But just as the Macedonian troops assembled to cross into Asia Minor in the spring of 336 B.C., Philip was assassinated and **Alexander III** took command of the invasion.

ALEXANDER THE GREAT (330 BC)

Philip's son, **Alexander** followed in his father's footsteps by consolidating Macedonian rule over Greece and pursuing a campaign against Greece's arch enemy, Persia.

For Alexander and his father, the defeat of Persia, the world's great superpower, was considered the ultimate act of revenge and defiance. For decades the imperious Persians had suppressed local revolts and threatened to overthrow the Greek city-states.

Alexander and his mostly Macedonian army began its attack of Persia in 334 B.C. at the Granicus River. This victory allowed him to march to the city of Gordium[22] and then to Issus where he defeated the army of Darius III, the king of Persia (although the king eluded capture).

---

[19] According to legend, a messenger (Pheidippides) ran more than 20 miles from Marathon to Athens to announce the defeat of the Persians before dying of exhaustion. His feat gave us the term "marathon," now applied to any long race or endurance contest.

[20] Athenians and Spartans united to form the Hellenic League with Sparta in charge of the army and Athens the navy.

[21] In 449 B.C., Persia and Athens signed the Peace of Callias.

[22] According to legend, in Gordium Alexander came across a complex knot tied around an ox cart that had been dedicated to the Greek god, Zeus. It was believed that whoever could untie the knot would become the master of Asia. When Alexander couldn't untie the knot himself, he drew his sword and cut through it in one stroke. Today the term "Gordian knot" means a perplexing puzzle and "cutting the Gordian knot" describes a quick, bold solution for a complex problem.

Two years later, Alexander liberated **Egypt** from Persian rule and was crowned **Pharaoh** (considered the son of a god).

Alexander, who was fascinated with Persian history, culture and dress, promoted the melding of Greco-Macedonian (Hellenistic) and Persian customs in the territories he conquered by leaving local Persian rulers in power and encouraging the flow of ideas between the regions. To reinforce the synthesis, Alexander even instructed 10,000 of his men to marry Persian women in a mass wedding ceremony.

Alexander's ambition to rule the world eventually led him to embark on a fateful campaign through present-day Afghanistan, Pakistan and across the border of India but the expedition proved to be too demanding for his army. His troops refused to accompany him beyond the Indus River Valley, forcing him to return to Persia. Three years later (323 B.C.), Alexander died in Babylon.

SELEUCIDS

After Alexander's death in 323 B.C., his vast empire was divided among his generals with Asia being passed on to General **Seleucus Nicator** (from where the name "Seleucids" comes). However, **Seleucus Nicator** and his successors didn't share Alexander's admiration of Persian culture. Instead, they reversed Alexander's efforts to blend eastern and western cultures by replacing local indigenous political and military leaders with elite Greek/Macedonians and favoring Greek customs over Persian. Their prejudices caused local resentment and provoked resistance to Macedonian rule.

Among the alienated groups were the Parthians, a group of nomads from central Asia related to the Scythians.

PARTHIANS (141 B.C. – A.D. 224)

The Parthians first became independent of Seleucid rule in remote areas of northern Persia around 250 B.C. under King **Arsaces.**

By the time Parthian leader **Mithridates I** had taken power in 171 B.C., the Seleucid Empire had become weak from internal power struggles and local rebellions. The post-Alexandrian Seleucids were also doomed economically when the Parthians captured Herat (in present-day Afghanistan) and cut off trade along the lucrative Silk Road between China and the Seleucids in the west.

For the next few decades, the wealthy Parthians (who spoke a Middle Persian language called "Pahlevi"), seized territory from as far east as present-day Pakistan to Israel in the west.

SASSANIDS (A.D. 224-A.D. 650)

Like the Seleucids before them, though, the Parthians became weak from internal rivalries and constant battle against the Romans (who had replaced the Greeks as the principal Western rival). They were finally defeated at the **Battle of Hormuz** in A.D. 224 by **Ardashir I**, a vassal[23] of the Parthian

---

[23] Vassal: one who receives protection and land from a lord in return for homage and allegiance.

6

king and a descendant of an **Achaemenid** priest called **Sassan**.

As ancestors of the Persian **Achaemenids**, the **Sassanids** claimed to be the legitimate heirs to the Persian Empire and endeavored to restore the empire's glory. After eliminating any remaining vestiges of Greek culture, the Sassanid rulers resurrected Persian traditions, reinstated **Zoroastrianism** as the state religion and persecuted adherents to all other faiths, including Christians.[24] The ruler adopted the Persian title of *shahanshah* ("king of kings").

In just a few years, the Sassanid Empire had become strong enough to challenge the Roman Empire[25] and for the next four centuries, the two superpowers engaged in endless battles that eventually left both empires too weak to resist the onslaught of the Islamic Arabs.

ARABS (A.D. 650)

In Arabia, a new religion called **Islam** ("submission" to God) based on spiritual revelations received by a Meccan caravan-leader called**Mohammed,** was rapidly spreading. The adherents, or *Muslims*, believed that Mohammed was the last in a succession of prophets that included Abraham, Moses, John the Baptist, Jesus and others sent by God to convey God's message.

When Mohammed died in 632, the Islamic community (or *umma*) was led by **Abu Bakr** (632-634), his elected successor (or *caliph*), who consolidated Islamic rule throughout the Arabian Peninsula (present-day Saudi Arabia).

Two years later **Abu Bakr** died and was replaced by **Umar ibn al Khattab** (634-644) who defeated the Roman Byzantines in **Palestine** and won a series of military victories in Egypt, Syria and Mesopotamia (present-day Iraq). In most of the vanquished territories inhabitants were given the choice of converting to Islam (which appealed to populations who felt oppressed and exploited by their overlords), paying a poll tax (*jizya*) or fighting. Islam quickly replaced the local religions while Arabic replaced local languages (among them Aramaic and Coptic) in most of the newly Islamic lands. But the Muslims were not secure as long as the formidable **Byzantine** and Persian empires continued to hover on their doorstep. Under Umar's leadership, therefore, the Muslims prepared to fight the **Sassanian** armies.

Beginning in 636, the Muslims won a number of victories over the Persian Empire. At the conclusion of the four-day-long **Battle of Qadisiya** in 637, they took control of the Sassanid capital of **Ctesiphon** and soundly defeated the Sassanids in **Nahavand** in 642.

---

[24] The persecution of Christians in the Sassanid Empire increased when Christianity became the official religion of their enemy, the Roman Empire in 381 under **Emperor Theodosius**.

[25] The supremacy of the Roman Empire had begun to decline after the death of Marcus Aurelius in A.D. 180 and was split into a western portion and an eastern portion centered around its capital city of Byzantium (present-day Istanbul, Turkey). By the 6th century, the western portion had fragmented into small self-sufficient Germanic kingdoms while "Byzantium" (the eastern Roman Empire) traded and fought with the Parthians and later the Sassanids.

Initially, the native population of Persia welcomed the egalitarian, tolerant Arabs over the class-conscious, bankrupt Sassanid rulers, although mass conversions to Islam didn't take place until the ninth century and only the elite adopted the Arabic language while most of the population continued to speak Persian.

SHI'ISM

After Caliph Umar's death in 644 at the hands of a Persian assassin, a selection committee chose **Uthman ibn Affan,** a member of the controversial Umayyad clan — once rivals of Mohammed's **Quraish** family — to succeed him.

The decision was particularly disappointing to a small group of people who believed that leadership over the Muslim community should have been passed to a blood-relative of the prophet. Specifically, they felt that **Ali,** Mohammed's cousin and son-in-law was the rightful heir to the **caliphate.**

In the first decade of **Uthman's** *caliphate* (or "rule"), the Islamic Empire grew to include Morocco in North Africa, Afghanistan in the east and Armenia and Azerbaijan in the north. The last few years of Uthman's rule, though, was plagued by tribal factionalism, local corruption and rebellion that resulted in **Uthman's** murder by mutineers from Egypt in A.D. 656.

In place of Uthman, the Muslim leaders appointed the prophet's cousin **Ali ibn Abi Talib,** but his reign as the Muslim community's fourth caliph was challenged.

Among contenders for the position was the Syrian governor and relative of murdered caliph Uthman, **Muawiya ibn Abu Sofian**. Muawiya, who had built up a formidable army of his own to counter the Byzantines in Syria, refused to acknowledge Ali's leadership and criticized the fourth caliph for failing to bring Uthman's killers to justice.

When Ali didn't forcefully condemn Muawiya's insubordination, a group of former supporters called the **Kharijites** turned on Ali and assassinated him in 661.

Muawiya took over the now vacated caliphate and appointed his son, **Yazid I**, as his successor — thereby turning the elected post into a hereditary dynasty (named the **Umayyad Dynasty** after the clan to which he and Uthman belonged).

The rivalry between Muawiya and Ali and their followers passed to the next generation when **Yazid** became the caliph upon his father's death in A.D. 680.

Ali's followers (called the **Shi'at Ali** — the "party of Ali" – or simply, the **Shi'as**) rejected Yazid's authority opting to back Ali's son **Husayn** instead. The stand-off took a fateful turn on the 10th day (called **Ashura** or "the tenth") of the Muslim month of **Muharram** in AD 680 when **Yazid's** military massacred a band of Husayn's followers in the city of **Karbala** (in present-day Iraq). The tragic event sealed the division between the Shi'as (the "party of Ali") and other Muslims called **Sunni** Muslims (from the word "Sunnah" a model of correct Islamic living based on the words and actions of Prophet Mohammed). (See section on Islam)

UMAYYAD DYNASTY (661-750)

The Umayyad Dynasty, founded by **Muawiya** in 661 and centered in Damascus, Syria, survived the Islamic schism in 680 and expanded the borders of Islamic power from Spain in the west to India in the east. The empire began to fall apart, however, under pressure from pious critics who considered the Umayyad rulers too secular, self-indulgent and weak to rule as well as the **Shi'ites** and **Kharijites** and others who continued to question the legitimate authority of the Umayyad leaders.

ABBASID DYNASTY (749-879)

As the Umayyad dynasty collapsed in a series of rebellions, a religious family claiming to be descended from Mohammed's uncle **Abbas** made a bid for power.

The **Abbasids** appealed to both the **Shi'as**, who were acceptant of the Abbasids' blood-line, and pious Muslims who were drawn by their moral character. They ruled as spiritual and political leaders after the death of the last Umayyad leader in the mid 8th century. [26]

In 762 the capital was moved from Damascus to the new city of **Baghdad** (in present-day Iraq) where great advances in literature, mathematics, astrology, medicine, art and philosophy helped usher in the **Golden Age of Islam**. At its height, the Muslim empire rivaled the **Byzantine Empire** in grandeur and sophistication.

But the Abbasid Empire was too vast and extravagant to maintain centralized power. Although on paper the Abbasid Empire remained in power until the **Mongols** conquered Baghdad in 1258, they were in competition with splinter dynasties that had developed within the empire from the first century of its existence.

While two of these groups, the Mongols and Timurids, swept through Persia, a peaceful Islamic Sufi[27] order under the leadership of **Sheikh Safi al-Din** was developing into a military and political powerhouse.

SAFAVIDS (1501-1722)

In his time, **Sheikh Safi** had been an important figure in the Mongol **Ilkhanate**,[28] but it was his sixth generation descendant, **Ismail,** who built

---

[26] Though the Abbasids were descended from Mohammed's uncle, Abbas, they were wary of the family directly descended from Ali, Prophet Mohammed's nephew and son-in-law. Once in power, the Abbasids severely restricted the family's activities eventually forcing the last of Ali's descendants, the "last Imam" according to Twelver Shi'ites, to go into hiding ("occultation") never to be seen again *(see Islam section for a thorough explanation)*.

[27] The Sufis are not an ethnic or religious group but a mystical Islamic movement. The Sufis rejected the worldliness of Islamic leaders and focused instead on a Muslim's direct relationship with God and a search for the mystical knowledge of God and his love.

[28] When Genghis Khan, the leader of the marauding Mongols, died in 1227, he divided his vast empire into Khanates to be ruled by his four sons. The Persian portion was inherited by his grandson Hulagu Khan in 1259 who called it the *Ilkhanate* or "subordinate *khanate*" in deference to the Great Khanate of China ruled by his brother Kublai Khan. descendants ultimately succumbed to local pressure and converted to Shi'a Islam.

the **Safavids** into one of the most influential empires in Persian history.

In 1501, **Ismail** employed a tribe of Turkish warriors called the **Qizilbash** or "red-heads" to help consolidate his rule and help in the pursuit of territory for his Safavid dynasty. With the Qizilbash as allies, he was able to defeat the **Aq-Qoyunlu** or "white sheep" (a leftover Mongol tribe that had taken over parts of Persia in the wake of the declining Timurid empire) and began raiding Ottoman lands in Asia Minor.

Ismail, a **Shi'ite** by birth, and the Shi'ite Safavids were particularly eager to wrest control of the Shi'ite holy cities of **Karbala** and **Najaf** in Ottoman-controlled Iraq. In 1508, with the help of the **Qizilbash** who were themselves resentful of Ottoman taxation and attempts to settle them, the Safavids took Baghdad instigating an ongoing rivalry with the Turkish Ottoman Empire.

To further distinguish his empire from that of the Sunni Ottomans and Sunni Uzbeks, Ismail declared Shi'ite Islam the official religion of Persia and forced all reluctant constituents to convert. By the end of the Safavid reign in the 18th century, a Shi'ite theocracy[29] had been firmly established in Persia and religious leaders had become an important force in the government.

> ## OTTOMAN EMPIRE
>
> The Ottoman Empire, or "Ottoman Sublime State" as it was known, was founded in the late 13th century by **Osman I**, a chieftain ("*bey*") of a Turkish tribe based in Anatolia (present-day Turkey). In 1453, the Ottomans captured the city of Constantinople, the capital of Christian Byzantine Empire, and renamed it Istanbul. At its height in the 16th century, the **Sunni Muslim Ottoman Empire** stretched from the Caspian Sea in the east to Hungary in Europe and south to include parts of North Africa. After defeat by the Allied Western powers at the end of World War I, the Empire dissolved into a number of European-designed independent states including Iraq, Jordan, Syria, Lebanon and Israel.

Many of Ismail's diplomatic and military conquests, though, did not survive after his death in 1524. The weakness of the new government[30] provoked the Qizilbash to rebel, allowing the Uzbeks and Ottomans to recapture territory lost to the Safavids a few years earlier.

The Safavid empire was finally restored to glory, however, with the accession of **Shah Abbas Bozorg** ("King Abbas the Great") in 1587.

One of Abbas's first moves as Shah was to lessen the Safavid reliance on the **Qizilbash** soldiers by creating a paid military that was answerable only to the central government. Knowing that he couldn't fight on two fronts at once, Abbas made peace with the Ottomans and concentrated on the eastern border, holding back Uzbek incursions.[31] Once the Uzbeks were subdued, Abbas turned on the

---

[29] Ismail had positioned himself as an infallible semi-divine figure.

[30] Ismail's son, Tahmap was only 10 when he began to rule. Tahmap's son, Ismail II was a murderous megalomaniac who blinded or killed most of his family members and his successor, Mohammed.

[31] The Safavids easily recaptured Herat during the chaos that followed the death of the Uzbek khan in 1598.

Ottomans, recapturing Tabriz in 1605 and reclaiming Baghdad in 1623.

Shah Abbas's successes against the Ottomans attracted the attention of the Europeans who had themselves been threatened by the Ottomans on their eastern borders and longed to bypass the Turks to conduct trade with Asia. With European cooperation and support,[32] Persia became one of the most lucrative centers of trade between east and west.

Abbas had been an insecure ruler who feared that his sons would depose him as he had done to his own father. To prevent such a reoccurrence, Abbas killed his oldest son and kept his other sons sheltered and uneducated in the harems. When his son and successor, **Safi** came to power, he was out of touch with the empire and had had no governing experience. It wasn't long before the Ottomans took Baghdad a final time,[33] the Qizilbash reignited their rivalry and the Safavid empire disintegrated.

While the Shahs and nobility had been over-indulging in the riches of the empire, Shi'a scholar-priests (the *ulema*) were becoming more powerful by claiming that the rampant corruption and decadence was God's punishment for endowing impious rulers with the authority to run the state. Instead, the *ulema* proclaimed that only religious scholars (*Mujtahid*) who were well-versed in **Sharia law** (Islamic law) were qualified to hold governing positions. In an attempt to reverse the damage done, the *ulema* strictly enforced Shi'ism and persecuted those who didn't observe the faith.

The dominance of Shi'a clergy and practices provoked a revolt by Sunni Muslims in the empire, culminating in a brutal takeover by Sunni Afghans in 1722. The Afghans under **Mahmoud Khan**, an Afghan chieftain from the Ghilzai family and then his cousin Ashraf, ruled Persia from 1722 to 1729.

NADIR SHAH

To break the power of the Safavids, the Afghan chieftain Mahmoud Khan orchestrated the killing of thousands of Safavid princes before he was killed by his own men in 1725. His cousin held the crown for a few more years but he was not prepared to battle the "Napoleon of Persia," **Nadir Shah** – a Persian fighter from the Turkic **Afshar** tribe employed by the **Safavids**.

With the Afghans defeated and the **Safavid crown restored,** the new Shah, **Tamasp II,** sent Nadir Shah to put down another rebellion in Qorosan. While Nadir was occupied in the east, however, Tajmasp II embarked on a disastrous campaign against the Ottomans and lost Georgia and Armenia in a humiliating peace treaty as a result.

By 1736, Nadir Shah had recaptured the lost territory, consolidated his position and ascended the throne himself.

---

[32] The British helped Persia break the Portuguese monopoly on maritime trade through the Persian Gulf by expelling the Portuguese from Bahrain and the island of Hormuz

[33] Baghdad remained in Ottoman hands until after World War I.

While serving as the head of the new **Afshar Dynasty**, **Nadir Shah** won a number of battles against the Ottomans. He captured Kabul (in Afghanistan) and marched to India where he plundered the great Indian treasures of the **Mughal** Emperors. Among the valuable spoils were the great **Koh-i-Noor** diamond and the **Peacock Throne** – which thereafter symbolized Persian imperial power.

In his later years, though, **Nadir** grew greedy, despotic, intolerant and paranoid. Suspecting that his own son was plotting against him, Nadir Shah had him blinded, and then executed the nobles who had witnessed the crime.

The empire fell into disarray after his death when his descendants quarreled among themselves and competed with nobles from the influential **Zand** and **Qajar** clans for power.

ZAND DYNASTY
After about a decade of anarchy, **Karim Khan Zand,** a former general under Nadir Shah, rose victoriously to head the new but short-lived Zand Dynasty. Karim Khan was a compassionate ruler who preferred the title *vakil ar-ra'aayan* (or "Peasants Regent") to "shah." He was also the first leader to open Persia to foreign influence by allowing the **British East India Company** (which had been created to manage Britain's economic and military relations abroad) to establish a trading post in the Persian Gulf port city of Bushehr.

But the empire didn't last long after his death in 1779.

QAJARS
In the decade after Karim Khan's death, five Zand rulers jostled with tribal leaders and other groups for the crown, leaving the country in a chaotic state. Order was finally restored when **Afgha Muhammad Khan**, a eunuch from the Azari **Qajar** tribe, defeated the last **Zand** ruler outside the city of Kerman in 1794 and made himself the overlord of the country. But the Qajars' reign, which lasted **until 1925**, was frequently deemed the most disastrous, damaging period in Iranian history.

Europe in the 18th and 19th centuries
The Qajars ruled in a period of great change. The Christian **Crusades** had exposed the West to jewels, spices and silk. Sea travel had become easier, faster and safer. As a result, maritime commerce took the place of land-based trade – consequently bypassing a number of Persian cities that relied on trade for their survival.

In the late 1700s, Europe had experienced an **industrial revolution** that drastically altered the social, economic and military structure of Europe. Cities began to grow. Capitalism and a free-market based economy replaced feudalism and hereditary privilege. Artisans were put out of work because they could not compete with manufactured goods that were cheaper and of higher quality. And factories produced and supplied the Europeans with better and deadlier weapons, giving them a great military advantage over less developed nations.

By the 1800s, Western nations were more technically advanced, better armed and wealthier than their eastern counterparts. And with the development of industrialism, they were in greater need of raw materials and overseas markets in which to sell their products. The new demands created a burst of imperial activity.

Britain

By the 19th century, the British had colonized such a large swath of land[34] that it was claimed that "the sun never sets on the British empire." But their greatest possession, the "jewel in the crown" of the empire, was India.

India was especially valuable to the British because of its lucrative trade, because of the troops India provided and because occupation of the territory gave the British a commanding position in South Asia. India had also become a symbol of Britain's might and prestige -- and the British were not about to give it up without a fight.

RUSSIA AND THE GREAT GAME

For 100 years the British and Russians engaged in a campaign of espionage and diplomatic intrigue (but not outright war) that became known as the "Great Game." The countries situated between the British and Russian empires, meanwhile, became pawns in the conflict.

In the race to colonize the world, the Russians expanded eastward by absorbing Siberia. Their dream, though, was to reach the Persian Gulf and procure another outlet to the sea.

In order to protect their southern border (and perhaps to inch ever closer to the warm waters in the south), the Russians set their sights on the Persian-controlled city-states of Georgia, Armenia, Azerbaijan (northwest of Iran) and the Caucasus (present-day Kazakhstan, Uzbekistan, Turkmenistan, Kyrgyzstan, Tajikistan – northeast of Iran, bordering Afghanistan). And in a span of 15 years and two humiliating treaties[35] signed by the Qajar shahs, the Russians had successfully won control over the regions.

Russia's steady advancement towards India,[36] though, had been deeply disturbing to the British. With the Caucasus and key Central Asian countries in Russian hands, only Afghanistan and Persia remained between Russia and India, and the British did everything they could to ensure that Afghanistan and Persia remained strong enough to serve as buffers. In both countries the British worked to maintain strong, stable (although not necessarily popular or capable), regimes able to withstand the Russians that helped forestall rebellions that could destabilize and weaken countries.[37]

In Persia, that meant supporting the incompetent, profligate Qajar shahs.

---

[34] By 1921, Britain held sway over roughly ¼ of the world's population living on about 35% of the world's total land area.

[35] Treaties of Gulistan (1812) and Turkmanchai (1828).

[36] It was estimated that the Russians were encroaching at a rate of 55 miles a day in the 19th century. The British feared that the Russians would use East Persia or Afghanistan to stir up rebellions among their Indian subjects.

[37] The British even discouraged Iran from constructing railways fearing rail access would make the country even more valuable to the Russians and facilitate a Russian invasion.

QAJAR SHAHS

While Europe was becoming a capitalistic and industrial civilization, the Qajar dynasty had devolved into an impoverished, backward and fractionalized country. Trade towns had suffered from the rise of maritime commerce and small traditional Persian craftsmen couldn't compete with the cheaper, better quality goods produced and imported from factories abroad. The Qajar rulers, consequently, relied largely on taxation and sales of lucrative jobs for income.[38] Making matters worse, the self-serving Shahs were notorious for their lavish lifestyles, often spending great amounts of money to take their entire courts on long sojourns to Europe.

When tax revenues couldn't cover the costs of the empire, the Shahs first borrowed money — thereby saddling the country with enormous debts – and then sold off interests (concessions) in Persia to European buyers.

When **Shah Nasser al-Din** fell short of cash, he tried to sell exclusive rights to exploit all Iran's economic resources for a lump sum of 40,000 British pounds[39] but was forced to cancel the deal. A few years later (in 1890), the Shah gave a British company a monopoly over the country's tobacco trade[40] sparking a revolt by clerics (who issued a *fatwa* or *religious ruling* forbidding the use of tobacco), *bazaaris* (merchants), nationalists and others.

In 1901, the Shahs granted British national **William Knox D'Arcy** a 60-year concession for all oil exploitation rights throughout Persia (excluding the provinces bordering Russia). When oil was discovered in 1908, the British formed the **Anglo-Persian Oil Company** (forerunner of the British Petroleum Company or BP) earning D'Arcy and Britain a fortune.

By the beginning of the 20th century, the Qajar Shahs were so indebted to Britain and Russia militarily, politically and financially that they had become powerless.

When it looked like Germany was becoming more and more of a threat, the British and Russians decided to resolve their differences, end the **Great Game** and band together. As a condition of the resulting **Anglo-Russian Agreement**, Britain and Russia agreed to divide Persia into spheres of influence. Russia would have the exclusive right to pursue its interests in northern Persia, the British would have complete sway over the southern and eastern portion and the center would be left to the Iranians themselves.

CONSTITUTIONAL REVOLUTION

By that time, the Persian population was fed up with the excesses of the Qajar regime. The *bazaaris* resented high prices, internal tariffs and the loss of markets to foreign imports. Shi'ite clerics (who had close ties to the *bazaaris*) feared the growth of secularism and Western influence. And politically-minded Persians

---

[38] Governorships and subordinate positions were sold to the highest bidder at an annual auction.

[39] To Baron Paul Julius von Reuter in 1872.

[40] Tobacco was widely used by Persians and widely grown in the country. The deal undercut Persian tobacco farmers and raised the cost of tobacco.

influenced by worldwide trends[41] demanded the establishment of a parliament and the creation of a constitution. Almost the entire population was unhappy with the regime and they displayed their discontent in a general uprising in 1906.

Folding under the pressure, the Shah (**Muzaffaru'd-Din Shah**), finally agreed to form an elected Parliament or **Majles**. Within a year, the new Majles had produced a constitution which gave wide powers to the people. To satisfy religious interests, the constitution also declared **Twelver Shi'ism** the state religion and set up a committee of five *mujtahids* (religious scholars) to ensure that legislation conformed to Sharia (Islamic law).

Five days later, though, the Shah died and the dream of the constitutionalists died with him. With support from the British and Russians (who feared a constitutional government would be a threat to their interests), the Shah's successor, **Mohammed Ali Shah**, arrested and executed the leaders of the constitutional movement and destroyed the **Majles**. In response, in July 1909, Persian constitutional fighters marched on the capital of **Tehran**, forcibly deposed and exiled **Mohammed Ali** to Russia and placed his young son, **Ahmed Shah**, on the throne in his place.

WORLD WAR I

In 1914 war broke out between the British, Russians, French, Italians, Japanese and later the Americans (collectively called the Allied Powers) and the Germans, Ottoman Turks, Austro-Hungarians, Bulgarians (the Central Powers) . Initially, the Persian Shahs declared themselves neutral but the British and Russians, who needed Persia's oil for their naval ships and wanted to prevent the Ottoman Turks from getting their hands on the commodity, forced Iran to participate. For the duration of the conflict the warring parties turned Persia into a battlefield, pillaging cultivated areas, enlisting peasants to serve in their armies and destroying irrigation infrastructures. When peace was declared in 1918, more than 2 million Iranians had died from famine or violence and the government (which was still recovering from the constitutional revolution) was in shambles.

Britain had coerced the Persians into signing the **Anglo-Persian Agreement** of 1919 granting the British the right to run the country's army, giving them favorable trade rates and awarding them the right to employ expert advisers to manage Persia's finances (including paying Mohammed Ali Shah a stipend). In return, the British agreed to recognize Persian sovereignty and provide a two million pound loan.[42]

Consequences of WWI

World War I had ended in victory for the Allied Powers[43]. The Ottoman Empire, as a result, was reduced to the area of present-day Turkey with the rest of the for-

---

[41] By the end of the 20th century, Great Britain, France and the United States had become democracies. The Japanese had a constitution and, after 1905, Russia and the Ottoman Turks had developed parliamentary forms of government.

[42] The loan was widely viewed as the establishment of a British protectorate over Iran.

[43] Versailles Treaty of 1919.

mer Ottoman regions being distributed among the victors. France acquired a mandate over Syria and Lebanon, the Jewish Zionists were prominent in Israel and Great Britain controlled the new nation of Iraq.[44] As a concession to the Arabs who had helped the Allies during the war, Sunni Arabian kings were placed on the thrones of Syria and Iraq[45] — despite Iraq's Shiite majority.

The Germans languished over the crushing defeat and the burdensome demand of $33 billion in reparation payments. Within an atmosphere of deep humiliation and financial distress rose an apparent savior – Adolf Hitler, whose nationalistic Nazi Party dominated Germany until the end of World War II.

In Russia, meanwhile, a Revolution had taken place (1917) which had brought an end to Tsarist rule and introduced the communist Bolsheviks under Vladimir Ilyich Lenin.

With Germany, the Ottomans and the Russians temporarily fallen from the ranks of the world's geopolitical players, Britain emerged as the sole European super-power.

PAHLEVIS
Reforms
The Anglo-Persian Agreement of 1919 had aroused considerable opposition among the Persians who were already smarting from the destruction caused by World War I and centuries of misrule. With little popular support, the young and incompetent last Qajar ruler, Ahmad Shah Qajar, was powerless against the Persian Cossack Brigade officer, Reza Khan.

In 1921, **Reza Khan Mirpanj** (as he was then called) staged a coup by claiming that he was there to defend the monarchy from an imminent revolution by the Qajar government. At first Ahmed Shah Qajar made him Minister of War and then, in 1923, he was named Prime Minister. When the **Shah** went on vacation in 1925, Reza took over the government altogether and was proclaimed Shah by a constituent assembly thereby launching the **Pahlevi dynasty** that would last until 1979.

In his 16-year rule, **Reza Shah Pahlevi** aimed to make up for time lost under the Qajars by reforming and industrializing the country. Under his rule, the **Trans-Iranian Railway** was built[46] linking Caspian ports to the Persian Gulf and also about 14,000 miles of roads. Although uneducated himself, the **Shah** set up a public school system that offered free education for every male and female Iranian citizen. He also established the University of Tehran and sent some students abroad to continue their education.

He abolished all special rights granted to foreigners, abrogated the never-ratified 1919 Persian-Iranian treaty and funded a navy and air force in order

---

[44] Iraq was cobbled together from the Ottoman *vilayets* (provinces) of Kurdish Mosul, Sunni Arab Baghdad and Shiite Arab Basra.

[45] The British installed their puppet Faisal Hashem from Saudi Arabia as king of the Hashemite Kingdom of Iraq that lasted until Saddam Hussein's coup in the 1950s

[46] Previously the British prevented the building of railroads in Iran, see footnote 37.

to minimize foreign influence in the country.[47]

In a drive to modernize and secularize the country, the **Shah** abolished **Sharia** courts, established civil courts and introduced the modern solar calendar (the lunar calendar continued to be observed for Islamic rites). He also discouraged, and then, in 1935, outlawed public use of headscarves and the **chador** — the long black cloak worn by pious Muslim Iranian women.[48] The edict made it easier for modern women to enter the burgeoning workforce but forced Iranian women who chose to cover themselves out of modesty or due to religious conviction to stay home.

The **Shah** had envisioned the creation of a "new Iranian man" styled on Western ideals, Western dress and Western social customs.[49]

Germany

Along with his admiration for Western culture, Reza Shah was also purportedly fascinated with the rise of modern Germany. Seeing an alliance with the Germans as a strategic alternative to British and Russian influences, the Shah worked to curry favor with the German Nazi government, increased trade ties with that country and employed German advisors.

It has been theorized that the **Shah's** relationship with the Nazis (who claimed that their descent from the Aryans[50] endowed them with superior qualities), played a role in his 1935 decision to formally rename the country "**Iran**" – from the root "Aryan" — to emphasize the country's own Aryan roots.

The new name was considered more in line with the existing demographic and geographic borders of the country since "Persia" (the "land of the Parsa") only referred to a portion of the country (Pars).

WORLD WAR II

A couple of years after "Persia" formally became "Iran," **Germany** joined **Japan** and **Italy** in a coalition that would come to be known as the alliance of the **Axis Powers**. Germany then claimed that it needed more *Lebensraum* or "Living Space" and annexed Austria (1938), Czechoslovakia (1939), western Lithuania and Albania. After signing a non-aggression treaty with the Soviets (to prevent a two-front war), Hitler invaded Poland thereby provoking Britain and France to declare war on Germany. World War II had begun.

Initially, the Shah was able to stay out of the conflict by declaring Iran's neutrality (despite his open friendship with Germany). But when the Nazis invaded the Soviet Union in 1941, the Iranians were forced to choose sides.

---

[47] The **Shah** also introduced conscription, established military factories to produce arms and ammunition and increased military pay.

[48] The Iranian gendarmes were ordered to cut or tear off veils worn in public. The law was rescinded in 1941.

[49] Surnames were mandated. Men were encouraged to wear Western clothes. Western mores were taught in schools. Religious minorities were guaranteed equal protection under the law. The Shah also provided free medical treatment for the poor and wired all Iran's cities with electrical power.

[50] Please visit www.enisen.com to learn more about various interpretations of the word "Aryan."

The Soviets joined the **Allied Powers** (Great Britain, Canada, Australia and New Zealand — France had fallen to the German Nazis in June 1940 and the U.S. hadn't yet joined the war) in their demand that Reza Shah expel all Germans and place the Trans-Iranian railroad and port facilities at their disposal. The Allies didn't want the Nazis to get their hands on Iranian oil (needed especially to fuel Britain's navy) and planned to use the Trans-Iranian Railroad and Iran's new roads to transport goods and weapons from the sea to Soviet troops in the north (called the "Persian corridor.")

When the Shah refused, the Russians and British invaded Iran, forced Reza Shah into exile in South Africa and installed his 22 year-old son **Muhammad Reza Shah Pahlevi** as the country's new leader.

For the duration of the war, foreign troops monopolized Iran's roads and railways, preventing the transport of Iranian goods and food and wreaking havoc on Iran's economy.[51]

In May 1945, the Germans surrendered, ending the war. The Japanese surrendered in September after the U.S. dropped atomic bombs on Hiroshima and Nagasaki.

THE COLD WAR

The war had put a tremendous strain on Britain[52] which consequently emerged politically and economically weaker. Taking its place as a world superpower was the United States which had, conversely, benefited from stepped up production during the war. The United States also inherited Britain's role as Russia's adversary.

For the next five decades, the United States and the Soviet Union and their allies engaged in a **Cold War** (so-called because the countries never engaged in actual combat) that affected nearly every world conflict from 1945 until the collapse of the Soviet Union in the 1990s.[53] One of the first U.S./U.S.S.R. crises took place in Iran.

Iran after World War II

In December 1943, Britain (represented by Prime Minister **Winston Churchill**), Russia (under **Joseph Stalin**) and the United States (led by President **Franklin Delano Roosevelt**) signed the **Tehran Declaration** pledging that all the participating nations would withdraw their troops from Iran and help the country recover. Only the Soviets didn't retreat as promised.

The Soviets under Stalin had hoped either to annex Iran or to cause it to shatter into smaller, less threatening states. To accomplish this, the Soviets backed the creation of a communist party in Iran (the **Tudeh** or "Masses" Party) and

---

[51] Iran experienced widespread famines as a result and inflation that at times reached 450%.

[52] After Germany invaded France and before the Russians and Americans joined the war, Britain was left to fight the Axis Powers alone.

[53] The Cold War virtually divided the world into two hostile camps supported by either the the Soviet Union or the United States.

tried to stir separatist movements among Iran's Kurdish and Azeri populations.

Stalin's troops finally left Iran in May 1946 after U.S. **President Harry S. Truman** (elected 1945) threatened to deploy the U.S. military to force the Soviets to withdraw.

Unrest

With the trials of the war behind them, the Iranians turned again to national issues. By that time, the new **Shah** was on his way to regaining autocratic power and tried to maintain it by rigging the 1946 **Majles** elections. After an assassination attempt, he cracked down on opponents, declared martial law and banned political parties, including the socialist Tudeh Party.

The **Shah's** actions triggered unrest by a broad spectrum of Iranian citizens. Intellectuals and Majles deputies objected to government corruption, manipulated elections, autocratic rule and the loss of civil rights (newspapers were censored or shut down, political gatherings were disbanded, opponents were intimidated, arrested and tortured, etc.). The lower classes suffered from inflation and famine (Iran was then one of the poorest countries in the world). Nationalists were fed up with continued foreign intervention. Tribal leaders objected to government extortion. *Bazaaris* (merchants) complained about crippling competition from foreign imports. And Muslim clerics (*mullahs*) were incensed over the government's decision to disband Shari'a courts, replace religious education with public schools, mandate civil marriage and other ceremonies and force young clerics to pass difficult exams in order to obtain licenses to preach.

All the affected parties joined in a coalition that centered on the **National Front Party** (*Jebhe Melli*), a nationalist organization founded by **Muhammad Mossadegh** and dedicated to ending the foreign presence in Iran – especially foreign oil companies.

MOSSADEGH AND THE NATIONALIZATION OF OIL

Since World War I, Britain had relied primarily on Iranian oil to fuel its ships, warplanes and automobiles and oil production and exports grew dramatically to meet the demand.[54] But as long as the British owned the **Anglo-Iranian Oil Company** (AIOC) they controlled the resource leaving Iran with little profit. In the wake of the post-WWII economic crisis, Iran needed the revenue more than ever.

The solution, maintained nationalist **Majles** members, was to nationalize Iran's oil industry and seize control of the British company (AIOC). Against the wishes of the Shah, the **Majles** named **Mossadegh** as Iran's new **prime minister** in 1951 to champion the cause. [55] True to his promises, Mossadegh enforced the **Oil Nationalization Act** shortly after coming to office effectively nationalizing

---

[54] In three decades, Iranian exports grew from 300,000 tons (in 1914) to about 16.5 million tons in 1945.

[55] The previous prime minister, Ali Razmara, had opposed oil nationalization. He was assassinated March 7, 1951 and Mossadegh was elected by Majles to take his place.

all of Iran's oil fields and expropriating AIOC's assets.[56]

The British responded by refusing to buy Iranian oil, freezing all Iranian assets in British banks and blocking all oil exports from the country thereby plunging Iran into economic turmoil.[57]

Despite the economic difficulties, **Mossadegh's** popularity soared in Iran – and plummeted abroad. The British needed Iran's oil and the U.S. feared that Mossadegh (who was by 1952 the undisputed ruler of Iran) was becoming too friendly with its Cold War enemy, the Soviet Union.[58]

When diplomacy failed, the British and U.S. resorted to covert actions to depose the prime minister and re-establish a more stable, friendly government.

In August, 1953, U.S. and British secret service agents (the **CIA** and **M16** respectively) carried out a secret plot code-named **Operation Ajax** to destabilize the government by fomenting disturbances between supporters and opponents of Mohammed Reza Shah.

The coup was completed by the Iranian military under **General Fazlollah Zahedi** who was called in to restore order. With the help of covert agents, **Zahedi** engineered a riot in August 1953 that gave them a pretense for toppling Mossadegh's government.[59] Soon after that, the former prime minister was arrested, the Shah was flown back to Iran , **Zahedi** was proclaimed the new prime minister and the flow of Iranian oil to foreign countries was restored. From that point on, the Shah relied on foreign aid and a heavy hand to stay in power.

WHITE REVOLUTION

After the Mossadegh incident, the **Shah** was more determined than ever to suppress all threats to his authority. To prevent another coup, he ensured that the government was made up of loyal supporters by closely controlling Majles elections in 1954 and replacing **Zahedi** with a string of subservient prime ministers.

The Shah launched a massive crackdown on all dissidents (by 1953 more than 1400 people were arrested) and banned all opposition parties. In their place, he sanctioned the formation of two official parties, the **Milliyun** and **Mardom** parties (and later **Iran Novin** in 1963) – all loyal to the government. And to keep an eye on all potential subversive activity, Shah Mohammed Reza created and employed an American-trained[60] secret intelligence force called the **Sazeman-I Ettalaat va Amniyat-I**

---

[56] The British company was compensated for its holdings.

[57] Iranian oil production fell from 660,000 to 20,000 barrels a day. Oil had been Iran's biggest export.

[58] Mossadegh had enacted a number of socialist reforms and was very close to the socialist Tudeh party which received backing from the Soviets.

[59] By the time he was deposed, Mossadegh had effectively become dictator of Iran and his popularity was eroding. Nevertheless, Iranians maintained that the British and the United States had ousted a popular democratic government out of self interest (namely, oil). The image of Mossadegh as the martyred victim of American aggression later became a key rallying point for Iran's future leader, Ayatollah Khomeini.

[60] The United States had helped Iran organize a modern intelligence service in order to keep an eye on Soviet activity.

Keshvar, the National Organization for Intelligence and Security or **SAVAK**

To regenerate Iran's economy and to bolster his regime, **the Shah** cultivated a symbiotic relationship with Britain and the United States. The Americans saw Iran as a bulwark against the Soviets[61] and felt it was in their interest to stabilize the government by providing the country with economic aid. The Shah, in turn, used the funds to buy American weapons and equip the military (in part to guard against internal threats).

After relations with Britain were restored in 1953, the embargo was lifted and revenues from oil began to pour in.

With his power effectively restored and the economy in an upswing (with help from American aid and oil revenues), the Shah turned his attention to domestic issues.

Beginning in 1963, the Shah endeavored to modernize Iran by launching a number of far-reaching reforms collectively called the **White Revolution**. At the cornerstone of the movement was the **Land Reform Act** which forced landowners to sell property in excess of one village. At the time, Iran's agriculture had been firmly in the hands of a small group of landowners and operated in a feudal manner.

> **SAVAK**
>
> SAVAK was created in 1957 with help from American secret service agents who had intended to employ the agency to spy on the Soviets. Instead SAVAK was used initially to round up members of the outlawed **Tudeh Party** (a socialist organization that had supported **Mossadegh**) and then to monitor all potential opponents (i.e. journalists, students [in Iran and abroad], labor unions etc.) SAVAK had the power to arrest and detain suspected persons indefinitely and was known to routinely torture subjects in detention centers (e.g. Evin Prison). After the fall of the **Shah** in 1979 the role of SAVAK was largely taken over by the religiously motivated **Ministry of Intelligence (SAVAMA)**.

In order to give workers, farmers, religious minorities and women greater representation in the government, the Shah reformed electoral laws. Elected officials were now allowed to take an oath on the holy book of their choice and women were granted complete suffrage in 1963.

In the 1960s, the regime also founded a large number of universities and initiated the **Literacy Corps** program that gave men who had finished secondary school (usually urban youth) the option to teach uneducated children in the countryside instead of serving two years in the army.

Other reforms were later enacted to help educate the populace and improve health services. Rural courts of justice were also established, waterways, forests and pastures were nationalized, state factories were privatized. The government also financed heavy industry projects and introduced profit-sharing for industrial workers.

---

[61] In 1971, Nixon deemed Iran and Saudi Arabia "twin pillars" in the effort to contain Soviet influence in the Middle East.

The reforms were initially welcomed by peasants and industrial workers but the rest of the population was unhappy with the regime.

POPULAR DISCONTENT

After the fall of **Mossadegh**, many Iranians saw Mohammed Reza Shah as America's puppet who, like the **Qajar** rulers of the 19th century, was selling Iran's sovereignty to foreigners for financial rewards. Many believed that the Americans were responsible for the Shah's modernization drive that only succeeded in making the rich richer.[62] The perception was reinforced in 1964 when **the Shah** approved a law that gave all Americans in Iran diplomatic immunity (a standard international procedure). Moreover, the Shah was using American-bought weapons and employing the CIA-backed SAVAK to keep the population in line.

When Iran's economy started to falter in the late 1950s, discontent grew. The influx of oil money, imports and financial aid had led to serious inflation.

Middle class workers (doctors, lawyers, civil servants etc.) saw their salaries drop, and price controls crippled *bazaaris* (merchants). Thousands of *bazaaris* were fined or jailed as a result of an anti-profiteering campaign. Lower income Iranians saw the gap growing between themselves and the super rich (whose money came through corruption and favors) and watched as luxury items they couldn't afford flooded the markets.

As they suffered, the aggrieved Iranians watched as the government continued to spend freely on the military (with no apparent external threat to justify the expenses) and mismanaged the Persian economy. One of the tipping points was the Shah's decision to host an extravagant $200 million party to celebrate the 2500th anniversary of the Persian Empire in 1971 while some provinces were experiencing famines.

The **White Revolution** had failed to live up to expectations. Landlords with connections managed to evade the Land Reform laws or were able to keep the most productive tracts and the new smaller landowners weren't able to get loans for equipment or supplies, forcing them to sell land back to the large landowners.

Despite the efforts of the Literacy Corps, 60% of the population was still illiterate and there were not enough schools to fulfill the promise of free universal education. Many of those who were able to complete school, moreover, found there were not enough places in universities to complete their education. Those who did get into college dealt with poor academic standards and poor housing and graduates couldn't find jobs.

Clergy

By far the most vociferous opponents of the White Revolution were the clergy. Many of the reforms had jeopardized their authority as religious leaders and others seemed to contradict Islamic dogma.

---

[62] The "White Revolution" -- so named because no blood was shed -- was described in the preamble of the 1979 constitution as a "step intended to stabilize the foundations of despotic rule and to reinforce the political, cultural and economic dependence of Iran on world imperialism."

The land reforms deprived many clerics and their patrons of their land for instance, while reforms in law and education undermined their roles as Islamic jurists and religious educators. Moreover, the Shah had created a **Religion Corps** that operated much like the Literacy Corps, by sending students to villages to educate Iranians in the state-sanctioned version of Islam.

The regime treated the clergy as a challenge to central authority. Like other subversive elements, clerics were monitored and harassed by security forces and hundreds were arrested, tortured and even killed by the regime.

The drive towards modernization and, by extension, westernization, flew in the face of Islamic ideals. Women's suffrage (in 1952) and the campaign to get women to join the workforce conflicted with traditional Islamic gender roles. The Shah's tolerance for religious minorities seemed to belittle Iran's Shi'a Muslim character, and the Shah's relationship with Israel was a betrayal of the Muslim Palestinian cause.

In reaction, the clergy accused the secular regime of being anti-Islam and argued that the institution of the monarchy itself was inconsistent with Islamic principles: that is, that only clerics well-versed in Islamic law could be considered legitimate leaders.

The clerics arguments were eagerly embraced by a new class of Iranians who had turned to traditional Islam for refuge in an unstable atmosphere. Peasants who had been displaced from the countryside to the cities found familiarity and comfort in the mosques, while others turned to Islam in reaction to modernization western trends (which seemed to threaten Iranian cultural values and identity). The mosque, moreover, was one of the few places where Iranians could feel free from the ever present eyes of the SAVAK. And since all rival political parties were outlawed, religious assemblies provided one of the only forums in which to exercise dissent. Even Iranians who weren't religious to begin with saw the practice of Islam as a form of defiance against the fiercely secular regime.

KHOMEINI

By the 1970s, the Islamic opposition was personified in **Ayatollah**[63] **Ruhollah Khomeini**, a Shi'a Muslim cleric and spiritual leader to many Shi'a Muslims.

Khomeini's popularity began to grow after he was arrested by the Shah's regime in 1964 for stating that the regime's basic aim was to oppose Islam and the existence of the religious class.[64] The arrest set off a riot joined by tens of thousands of Iranian teachers, students, *mullahs* (clerics), shopkeepers, National Front members and others and ended in the death of hundreds

---

[63] See box on page 42 for an explanation of the Shi'a Muslim title, "Ayatollah.."

[64] In 1962, Khomeini objected to a law allowing municipal officials to be sworn into office using the holy scripture of their choice thereby allowing Christians, Bah'ais and other non-Muslim Iranians to serve in office. He also criticized the government for "surrendering Iran's independence and sovereignty in exchange for a $200 million loan "that would only benefit the Shah" and submitting to imperialist powers through his "American-inspired" White Revolution..

of protesters at the hands of government troops.

After his release from prison 8 months later, Khomeini, by then a national figure, criticized the government's decision to grant diplomatic immunity to American soldiers and families stationed there. Americans in the United States, Khomeini claimed, would receive greater punishment for killing a dog than they would if they killed a religious leader on Iranian streets.[65] This time, Ayatollah Khomeini was exiled to Turkey and then to Iraq.[66]

The Ayatollah continued to attack **the Shah** and organized supporters from his new home in the Shi'ite holy city of Najaf in Iraq via sermons that had been recorded on cassette tapes and smuggled into Iran by religious students. The lectures delivered between 1969 and 1970 were later published as a book titled **"Velayat-e Faqih"** ("The Rule of the Islamic Jurist").[67]

Rather than diminishing his prestige, Khomeini's exile helped elevate him to an almost mythical status, making him the most influential figure in the approaching Islamic revolution — although other guerrilla movements within Iran were also active.

GUERRILLA MOVEMENTS

In 1965, the **Mujahideen-e-Khalq (MEK)** ("People's Struggle") was founded by religious militants and members of the **National Front** (Mossadegh's party) to wage a terrorist campaign against the government. The Mujahedin-e-Khalq actively supported the Ayatollah Khomeini in 1978 and 1979 and mobilized hundreds of thousands of students, workers and young army officers to participate in the Islamic Revolution. The organization also supported the seizure of the U.S. Embassy in Tehran in 1979.[68]

Refugees from the **Tudeh** and other Marxist groups also united to form the **Fed'iyan-e Khalq** (People's Guerrillas) organization. Both organizations used similar tactics in an attempt to overthrow the regime.

---

[65] By 1978 there were more than 40,000 Americans in Iran engaged in business or in military training and advisory missions. Criminals were referred to American disciplinary agents.

[66] Khomeini was first exiled to Turkey but, because that secular country forbade the Ayatollah from donning the cloak and turban worn by Muslim scholars, he moved to Najaf where he lived for the next 13 years.

[67] See box on Khomenei (pg. 33) for more on Velayat-e Faqih.

[68] The relationship between the new Islamic regime and MEK deteriorated when the regime refused to let MEK members participate in the government because of their leftist ideology. An intense and deadly rivalry between the Marxist organization and the Islamic government developed as a result. In 1981, MEK was driven out of Iran and resettled in Paris. From their new European base, the group attracted members and financial support from exiled Iranian politicians, Iranian families whose relatives had been executed by Khomeini's regime and other disenfranchised and embittered expatriates. MEK supported Iraq at the end of the 8-year war against Khomeini's Iran and moved its headquarters to Iraq in 1987. With the support of Iraqi President Saddam Hussein, MEK continued to combat the Iranian regime through bomb attacks, assassinations and other aggressive operations. The U.S. cracked down on MEK activity during the 2003 Iraq war.

Pre-Revolutionary Political Timeline

Elamites (c. 2500 - 1200 B.C.)
Medes (c. 750-550 B.C.)
Achaemenids (550-330 B.C.)
Alexander the Great (330 B.C.)
Parthians (247 B.C. - A.D. 224)
Sassanians (A.D. 224-642)
Umayyads (649-876)
Seljuk Turks (1051-1220)
Mongols (1220-1335)
Tamerlane and Timurids (1380-1502)
Safavids (1502-1722)
Afghanistan (1722-1729)
Nadir Shah (1736-1747)
Karim Khan Zand (1747)
Qajars (1779-1925)
Constitutional Revolution (1906)
Pahlevis (1925)
   Reza Shah Pahlevi (1925-1941)
   Mohammed Reza Shah Pahlevi (1941-1979)
Islamic Revolution (1979)

***

Post-Revolutionary Political Timeline

Supreme Leader
Ruhollah Mousavi Khomeini (Jan. 1980 - Jun. 1989)
Muhammad Ali Hoseyn Khamenei (Jun 1989 - present)

Prime Minister
Mehdi Bazargan (Feb. 1979 - Nov. 1979)
Muhammad Ali Rajai (Aug. 1980 - Aug. 1981)
Mohammed Javad Bahonar (Aug. 4 - Aug. 30 1981)
Mir Hoseyn Mousavi (Oct. 1981 - Aug. 3, 1989)

President
Abolhasam Bani-Sadr (Feb. 1980 - Jun. 1981)
Muhammad Ali Rajai (Aug. 2 - Aug. 30, 1981)
Mohammed ali Hoseyn Khamenei (Oct. 1981 - Aug. 1989)
Ali Akbar Hashemi Rafsanjani (Aug. 1989 - Aug. 1997)
Mohammed Khatami (Aug. 1997 - Aug. 2005)
Mahmoud Ahmadinejad (Aug. 2005 - present)

ISLAMIC REVOLUTION

When American President **Jimmy Carter** took office in 1977, discontent among all socioeconomic groups in Iran was widespread and revolution was imminent.

The new U.S. president was committed to advancing human rights worldwide prompting the Shah to make concessions within Iran to stave off American pressure. In a show of good will, the Shah released more than 300 Iranian prisoners, relaxed censorship and made changes to Iran's court system.

Revolution – First Stage

The new freedoms, while welcomed by most Persians, also allowed opponents to publicly express their grievances. Middle-class intellectuals led by **Mehdi Barzagan**, head of the liberal, secularist, **Freedom Movement of Iran,** kicked off the revolution by demanding greater freedoms equal to that in Western Europe and the United States and insisting that the Shah rule in accordance with the constitution which placed limits on royal power and provided for a representative government. Later the demands included the end of the one-party system that had been introduced in 1974, freedom of the press and the freeing of political prisoners.

Revolution – Second Stage (Islamic Revolution)

On January 7, 1978, a week after **Jimmy Carter** had effusively praised the Shah during a visit to Iran,[69] the protest took a new turn in response to an editorial published in one of Iraq's leading newspapers, the **Ettelaat**,criticizing the Ayatollah Khomeini.

The article was widely believed to have been secretly penned by members of the Shah's secret service, **SAVAK**,[70] to discredit the Ayatollah by calling him a British agent, a closet homosexual and an alcoholic. The article outraged Khomeini's followers and prompted religious students and local supporters to demonstrate in the religious city of **Qom** where Khomeini had taught until 1963. The protesters attacked what they considered symbols of modernity, restaurants, movie theaters and girls' schools, provoking the police to intervene. In the end, eight people had been killed: 6 protesters and 2 police officers.

According to Shi'a Muslim tradition, deaths are mourned by friends and family members forty days after loved ones have passed away. In observance of this custom, 40 days later, on February 18th and 19th, the victims of the January uprising were publicly memorialized in services held at mosques throughout the country. The public gathering in the city of Tabriz turned violent resulting in the deaths of more than 100 demonstrators. Forty days later, the cycle continued as those martyrs were mourned causing another round of protests and repression. Stoked by Khomeini, who continued to issue directives from exile in Iraq, the demon-

---

[69] During the visit, Carter also expressed his deep personal friendship with the Shah, complimented the Iranian leader for the "respect, admiration and love your people bear you" and called Iran "an island of stability in one of the most troubled regions of the world."

[70] The Shah's secret police were also believed to have been behind the mysterious death of Khomeini's son in Najaf in October 1977.

strators continued to attack and burn what the mullahs regarded as symbols of moral corruption and Western influence including liquor stores, cinemas, luxury hotels, banks and governmental offices.

In order to accommodate his liberal critics, the Shah announced in August that parliamentary elections open to all political groups would be held in the spring of 1980.

The gesture didn't appease the demonstrators and violence continued -- including the burning of the **Rex Cinema** killing 400 movie-goers trapped inside. By early September the unrest had forced the government to freeze wages, unemployment was widespread, inflation was rampant and Iran's economy was in shambles.[71]

In desperation, on September 8, 1978 (later called "**Black Friday**" by the revolutionaries) the Shah imposed martial law and made the fateful decision to employ full force against the protesters. The carnage caused by the regime's tanks and heavy machinery effectively crushed any hopes of compromise.

A month later, the Shah tried to lessen **Khomeini's** influence in Iran by asking Iraqi president **Saddam Hussein** to curb the Ayatollah's political activity from his headquarters in Najaf, Iraq. Rather than complying with Hussein's demands, Khomeini moved his entourage to France where, ironically, he enjoyed even greater freedoms than he had in Iraq and worldwide media attention. From his home in a Paris suburb, Khomeini was able to incite civil disobedience in Iran and coordinate a general strike (relayed by the French media) that forced most of Iran's industries to be shut down in October 1978.[72] The strike was followed in December by a two-million-strong demonstration that paralyzed the country.

In one last attempt to pacify the people, Shah Mohammed Reza appointed a moderate, **Shapour Bakhtiar**, as the new prime minister and announced that he would be leaving on an "extended vacation."

After the Shah's departure, Bakhtiar dissolved Iran's hated secret service, SAVAK, released all political prisoners and on February 1, 1979, permitted Khomeini to return to Tehran.

Two weeks after the Shah's departure, **Ayatollah Khomeini** triumphantly returned to Iran from Paris (Feb. 1, 1979) and immediately declared Bakhtiar's government illegal.[73]

---

[71] In 1973-74, the price of crude oil had quadrupled and Iran's production had risen so high that it had become the fourth most important oil-producing country in the world. All of Iran's industries prospered as a result and living conditions greatly improved. But euphoric optimism and high expectations turned to discontent when the price of oil fell and sales to oil-buying countries dropped. By that time, the influx of foreign money had caused inflation to spiral out of control.

[72] Postal and bank employees went on strike as did oil workers, journalists, mineworkers, transportation crews and students.

[73] "This government represents a regime, whose leader (Mohammed Reza Shah) and his father (Reza Shah Pahlevi) were illegally in power. This government is therefore illegal." (speech by Khomeini). To Bakhtiar "The government of our choice relies on the nation's backing and enjoys the backing of God. If you claim that your government is legal, you must necessarily be denying God and the will of the nation."

The battle between supporters of the imperial regime backing Prime Minister Bakhtiar and pro-Khomeini demonstrators raged on for another month until Bakhtiar, recognizing that he had lost the support of Iran's armed forces, was forced to concede.[74]

Upon Bakhtiar's formal resignation, Iran was declared an Islamic republic[75] and Khomeini was appointed the country's political and religious leader for life, though, technically, governance of the country was left to **Mehdi Bazargan** who had been appointed the first prime minister of the revolutionary regime.

HOSTAGE CRISIS

Despite many obstacles, the Islamic Republic of Iran's first prime minister, **Mehdi Bazargan**, initially tried to improve Iran's economic and political situation by cultivating diplomatic ties with the United States.

But foreign relations between the two countries took a severe turn for the worse when American president **Jimmy Carter** agreed to let the Shah (then residing in Mexico) come to the United States to receive medical treatment for an advanced case of cancer.

The gesture, mixed with memories of America's involvement in the 1953 covert operation that toppled the popular **Mossadegh** regime and re-installed the Shah, infuriated the Iranian people who marched on Tehran by the thousands demanding the extradition of **Mohammed Reza Shah** from the U.S. so that he could face trial in his own country.

On November 3, 1979, a group of zealous students demonstrated their anger by attacking the United States Embassy and taking 52 of its American occupants hostage.

Ayatollah Khomeini greatly endorsed the takeover and two days later, **Mehdi Bazargan** resigned his post in opposition. His resignation demonstrated the victory of Iran's radical forces in the country over the moderates. Those who opposed the seizure were branded American accomplices or were accused of abandoning the revolution in a time of crisis while the radicals were lauded as loyal revolutionaries.

Under Carter's orders, the Americans retaliated by freezing billions of dollars of Iranian assets held in American banks,[76] banning the import of Iranian oil and imposing sanctions. Nevertheless, the new Iranian regime calculated that the political benefits gained from the continued siege far out-

---

[74] By Feb. 12 Bakhtiar was in hiding and key points throughout the capital were in rebel hands.

[75] On March 30 and 31, 1979, a national referendum was held to determine the kind of political system to be established. The government reported that an overwhelming majority of the people (98%) voted in favor of an Islamic republic – the only choice on the ballot – and Khomeini proclaimed the establishment of the Islamic Republic of Iran on April 1, 1979.

[76] Funds were frozen to prevent Iranians from withdrawing the money en masse. Most, but not all of the funds were released after the hostages were released. Iranian politicians continue to demand the release of billions of dollars worth of assets that remain frozen in the U.S.

weighed the financial cost of severed relations with the United States.

The standoff between the Iranian hostage takers and the U.S. continued after the Shah had died (July 1980), after Iraq declared war on Iran in September, and continued through the U.S. presidential elections in November 1980. Carter's failure to free the American hostages had cost him the election (proving that the Iranians, themselves, could "topple" an American leader) and, adding insult to injury, the Iranians waited until moments after Jimmy Carter's successor, President **Ronald Reagan**, took his oath of office on January 20, 1981 before releasing the Americans they held captive.

By that time, the Iranians had become more concerned about the war against Iraq than the ideological battle with the Americans. The political isolation from both Western and Islamic countries as a result of the hostage crisis hurt Iran economically and prevented the country from acquiring much needed arms and ammunition.

Consequences
The 1979-1981 hostage crisis became a defining moment in U.S.-Iranian relations in the same way that the CIA-led operation against **Mossadeq** shaped the Iranian view of America. Jimmy Carter's inability and disinclination to use force to free the hostages also compelled Reagan and his successors to reassess America's military infrastructure and foreign policy.

IRAN-IRAQ WAR ("Iraq-Imposed War")

The rivalry between ethnically Persian Iran and Arab Iraq (once Babylonia, and the eastern edge of the Ottoman Empire) dates back to ancient times. From the 14th century until World War I, the three Ottoman *vilayets* or "districts" that eventually made up Iraq[77] served as a bulwark between the Ottoman and Persian Empires and, when the Safavids declared Shi'a Islam the state religion in the 16th century, the regions were divided along spiritual lines as well — although more than 60% of Iraq's population, mostly in the south-east, remained Shi'a.

The rivalry deepened politically in 1978 when the Iraqis under Saddam Hussein (then Iraq's powerful vice-president) complied with the Shah's request to expel the **Ayatollah Khomeini** from the holy city of **Najaf** in Iraq where he had been living in exile for the past 15 years. The slight wasn't forgotten when Khomeini became Iran's Supreme Leader a year later in the course of Iran's Islamic Revolution in 1979.

The Islamic Revolution posed a great threat to the regime of Saddam Hussein who had become president in July 1979. Its religious overtones threatened Hussein's secular government and he feared that the revolutionary spirit would provoke ethnic Kurds in the north and Iraq's majority Shi'ite population in the south to rise up against his Sunni Baathist regime. To thwart such an uprising, Hussein exiled thousands of Iraqi Shi'ites to Iran and quickly and brutally suppressed any dissension among the Kurds.

At the same time, Hussein saw an opportunity to take advantage of Iran's instability during its political transition and the weakness of its military (which had been decimated through regular purges of military officers once loyal to the former regime) in order to seize Iran's oil-rich, primarily Arab-populated Khuzestan province. Hussein had wrongly expected the Iranian Arabs to join the Arab Iraqi forces and win a quick victory for Iraq.

Hussein's official justification for declaring war on Iran originated from a long-standing dispute over access through the **Shatt-al-Arab** waterway, Iraq's main shipping route to the Persian Gulf.

Under the terms of the 1975 **Algiers Treaty**, Iraq agreed to place the border between Iran and Iraq in the middle of the **Shatt-al Arab** waterway in exchange for the Shah's promise to withhold support from Iraq's Kurds. Hussein rejected the treaty in September 1980, claiming that the arrangement had only been temporary and was valid only as long as the Shah was in power. A few days later, Iraqi troops embarked on a massive invasion of Iran.

War

At first, it seemed as if Iraq would easily defeat Iran despite Iran's greater size and population. Iraq's troops were better-trained, better-armed and confident.

---

[77] After World War I, the eastern Ottoman *vilayets* of Basra, Baghdad and Mosul were severed from the rest of the former Empire by the British to create "Iraq." See Roraback's Iraq in a Nutshell.

Iran's forces, in contrast, had been badly depleted and were led by inexperienced clerics. Morale among the remaining troops was low and the country's military equipment, vehicles and planes were old and in disrepair.

To supplement the regular forces and **Pasdaran, Khomeini** created a volunteer militia called the **Basij** (Haid-e Basij-e Mostazafan, or "mobilization forces") that attracted hundred of thousands of pious Muslims willing to become martyrs on the battlefield.[78] What the **Basiji** lacked in training and supplies, they made up in fanatical devotion and the "army of twenty million" as it was called, was deployed in large-scale "human-wave" assaults against the Iraqis.

In the early 1980s, the human-wave attacks proved to be effective, forcing the Iraqis to retreat and winning a small piece of Iraqi territory for the Iranians. But the tactic resulted in the loss of the lives of more than 100,000 men from landmines, gunfire and chemical weapons (which the Iraqis employed early in the war).

War of the Cities

For the first few years of the war the United States remained neutral. Memories of the hostage crisis discouraged the Americans from supporting Iran. And Saddam Hussein, whose record of human rights abuses and close relationship with the Soviets,[79] was hardly an American ally.

But the U.S. stance changed when Iran, considered the greater of the two evils, began to win occasional victories. The danger that Iran would overtake Iraq and its oil and spread the revolution to Jordan, Israel and other countries in the Middle East prompted the United States and its allies to aid Saddam Hussein. Along with receiving economic aid and intelligence, Iraq was also permitted to import weapons and missiles that could be fired as far as Iran's capital city, Tehran. The Iran-Iraq war had already taken its toll on Iranian citizens suffering from food and housing shortage and the effects of a strained economy. Now, the conflict (including the possibility of chemical warfare) was brought to their doorsteps.

Iran-Contra Affair

While the Iraqis (with Western aid) and Iranians were battling it out in a "war of the cities," U.S. president **Ronald Reagan** was embroiled in a political debate over the fate of seven American hostages being held in Lebanon by Iran-backed **Hezbollah** terrorists.[80] Like Carter before him, Reagan was being pressured to get the hostages freed without giving in to the demands of the captors.

Israel, in the meantime, was troubled by Iraq's successes in the Iran-Iraq war (Hussein's regime posed a greater threat to Israel than Iran was) and aimed to turn the tide back in Iran's favor by selling arms and ammunition to Iran. Before the transfers of requested American-made anti-tank and surface-to-

---

[78] Thousands of Iranian men and boys died walking as human waves straight into the line of fire or clearing minefields with their bodies to make a path for Iranian tanks.

[79] Iraq had signed a Treaty of Friendship with the Soviets in 1972.

[80] See "Terrorism" section.

air missiles were made, though, Israel was obliged to get American approval. In exchange for America's consent, the Iranians promised to compel the Hezbollah fighters to release the American hostages.

Adding even more controversy to the secret deal, profits earned from the sale of the American missiles were clandestinely diverted to the Nicaraguan **Contra** guerrillas then battling the **Sandinista** government.

Unfortunately for Reagan and the American officials involved in the covert operation, the whole affair was revealed in a November 3, 1986 story written in a Lebanese weekly news magazine and, soon after, picked up in the American press. The event became a domestic scandal in the United States and badly hurt America's reputation abroad. [81]

War ends
By 1988, the war had cost Iran and Iraq more than a million war casualties and left the economies of both countries devastated. For the Iranian people, the hardships of life during 8-years of war combined with disillusionment over the revolutionary government's inability to live up to its promises. In order to save the revolution, Khomeini reluctantly decided to accept a UN-sponsored ceasefire. [82]

On August 20, 1988, Iran and Iraq signed the UN Security Council Resolution 598 ending the war and restoring borders to their pre-war positions.

Consequences
The 8-year conflict had taken its toll on Iran. It was estimated that 100s of billions of dollars would be needed to repair the damage exacted on Iranian cities and infrastructure and the country's oil industry (which would have otherwise been tapped to pay for reconstruction) had been crippled by Iraqi bomb attacks on Iran's main oil-exporting port of **Khorramshahr** and the **Abadan** oil refinery[83] in Khuzestan. Inflation in Iran in 1988 had risen above 40%, unemployment was very high, and per capita income had dropped 40% since the 1979.

---

[81] Two senior members of Reagan's administration were convicted of a number of crimes, one committed suicide, six were pardoned and the president nearly faced impeachment proceedings. Internationally, it became evident that the U.S. was willing to capitulate to the terrorists to secure the release of hostages, and it exposed America's hypocrisy in condemning countries who sold military equipment to Iran while the U.S. was itself selling goods to Iran.
[82] Khomeini claimed the decision to accept Resolution 598 ending the war was for him more "deadly than poison."
[83] The world's largest oil refinery at the time.

AYATOLLAH KHOMEINI

Ruhollah Musavi Khomeini was born in September 1900 in the small town of Khomein outside of Tehran from where he gets his name. His family was descended from **Imam Musa al-Kazim**, the seventh in the line of twelve Imams who followed the ancestral line from the **Ahl al-Bayt** (Prophet Muhammad's family) and he was admired for his deep piety, austere, acetic lifestyle and his knowledge of Islam.

Khomeini had memorized the Koran at an early age and spent most of his youth studying Islamic law at traditional religious schools in Qom. By the time he was 50 years old, he had published essays on *fiqh* (Islamic jurisprudence) and had inspired enough followers to be considered an *ayatollah* or supreme religious leader.

Velayat e-Faqih
While in exile in Iraq, Ayatollah Khomeini penned a book (the "Velayat e-Faqih" or "Rule of the Islamic Jurists") outlining his beliefs regarding Islamic governance. According to Khomeini, all laws of the land should be based on the laws of Islam and adherence to those laws should be monitored by clerical authorities. The leader of an ideal Islamic Republic, he theorized, should be an Islamic Jurist ("*faqih*") elected by an assembly of clerics based on his supreme knowledge of Islamic law and ability to provide "right-minded" guidance.

Khomeini's family
Khomeini married a cleric's daughter who bore him two sons and three daughters (two more children died in infancy). His eldest son, Mostafa, died in 1977 in Iraq and his younger son, Ahmad died in 1995 under mysterious circumstances.

Khomeini's grandson, **Hossein Khomeini**, is a high-profile cleric and critic of Iran's current regime. After America's invasion of Iraq in 2003, Hossein Khomeini moved to Baghdad where he advocated the separation of church and state and denounced Iran's leaders as a "despotic religious regime reminiscent of the rule of the church during the Dark Ages in Europe. He claimed that "all those who came to power after the death of his grandfather exploited his name and that of Islam to continue their unfair rule." He also invited America to overthrow the clerical regime as it had done to Saddam Hussein's regime in Iraq.

SALMAN RUSHDIE AFFAIR

In the immediate post-war period, some social restrictions were lifted to ease public discontent and measures were taken to cultivate relationships abroad in order to attract badly needed foreign capital. But when loosened strictures on free speech invited too much criticism, and relations with the West (especially relations with the '**Great Satan**," the **United States**) became too friendly, Supreme Leader **Khomeini** decided to reassert his spiritual authority by issuing a *fatwa* (religious edict) calling on all Muslims to kill the Indian-born, British author of **The Satanic Verses**, **Salman Rushdie,** and all those involved in the book's publication and distribution (see sidebar). Translators and others associated with the book were taunted, injured or killed by zealous Muslims worldwide answering Khomeini's call and Rushdie was forced to live in hiding with round-the-clock security until the edict was lifted nine years later (although some hardline Muslims maintain that the *fatwa* is still active and some private organizations still offer huge rewards for Rushdie's death).

The Rushdie affair badly damaged Iranian-British relations until 1998 when Iran agreed to distance itself from the death-warrant.

SATANIC VERSES

"**Satanic Verses**" was denounced by the Ayatollah Khomeini and the Islamic community because of the book's little-disguised references to Quranic figures and stories and Rushdie's apparently heretical interpretations. In one portion of the book, for example, a character called the **Prophet Mahound of Jahilia** (a character seemingly representing the **Prophet Mohammed**), receives revelations of divine and "satanic verses"[a] from God. Mahound is later accused of altering the revelations to suit him. Panicked that he will be discovered, the character flees Jahilia for Yathrib (a reference to Prophet Muhammad flight from Mecca to Medina [Yathrib]). Mahound, who returns to Jahilia with many followers, is further accused of being obsessed with restrictive laws[b] while he was in Yathrib, some of which parallel Sharia, traditional Islamic law.

Muslim clerics particularly fear that since many of the stories closely resemble historical incidents and actual Quranic verses, uninformed readers would not be able to discern fact from fiction.

In chapter IV, Rushdie makes a political statement through a character that closely resembles Iran's bearded, turbaned Supreme Leader, the **Ayatollah Khomeini** (described as a "living stone" who is obsessed with purity and cleanliness). The exiled **Imam** in the book is carried by **Gibreel** to Jerusalem (just as Muhammad was said to have been taken on a "night journey" by the Angel Gabriel in the Quran) where he witnesses a popular revolution. In the scene (undoubtedly a characterization of the "human-wave attacks" in the Iraq-Iran war), the protesters march towards the soldiers 70 at a time. As they are gunned down, another 70 people climb over the bodies and are also shot. Mothers with covered heads push their sons to join the parade, to be martyrs themselves. "This isn't love" Gibreel weeps, "It's hate."

[a] The "satanic verses" are based on an Islamic legend that claims that Muhammad was tempted to make a deal with powerful merchants to stop teaching in return for wealth and prestige. He received verses from Satan that deceived him into conforming his religion to the traditional religion of Mecca by bringing in three former Meccan goddesses (al-Lat, al-Uzza and Manat). When Muhammad recognized the ruse and recanted the verses, the wealthy clans turned against him. The story is rejected by most Muslims.

[b] For example laws regarding the foods that were permissable to eat, how deeply they should sleep, what sexual positions were acceptable (sodomy, strictly forbidden in Islam, was listed as acceptable), what parts of the body could be scratched, how animals should be killed (in Satanic Verses they are supposed to slowly bleed to death, in the Quran, animals must be slaughtered quickly) etc.

KHAMENEI ASCENDS

By 1988 Khomeini was 86 years old and his health was declining. He knew that it was time to prepare the country for his succession and was aware that no candidates could match his charisma and authority and religious credentials. To preemptively strengthen his successor's position, therefore, Khomeini proclaimed that the authority of the Supreme Leader (Vali-ye faqih) was absolute.[84]

Khomeini had first designated **Grand Ayatollah Hossein-Ali "Gorbeh Nareh" Montazeri** to be his successor. Montazeri's criticism of Khomeini and the hardliners in the Islamic government and his denouncement of the institution of **Velayat-e faqih**,[85] though, made him an unsuitable candidate. Instead, **Seyyed Ali Hosseini Khamenei,** Iran's president since 1981 and a close confidante of Khomeini, was chosen. **Khamenei** was a high-ranking cleric but, unlike **Montazeri**, he hadn't yet reached the rank of **Grand Ayatollah** which, at the time, was a constitutional requirement to fill the post of Supreme Leader.

To accommodate Khamenei, Iran's constitution was changed to allow someone of a lower clerical rank to be elected leader of the Islamic Republic of Iran. He was later promoted to the appropriate rank though some Shi'ite clerics refused to acknowledge Khamenei's new clerical position contending that the rank of Grand Ayatollah must be earned.

Two days after Khomenei's death on June 3, 1989, the Assembly of Experts announced that Khamenei would be Iran's new Supreme Leader.

To counter any questions about his legitimacy serving as Iran's highest leader, Khamenei radically adhered to Khomeini's ideological principles. By assuming a conservative stance on issues pertaining to the Islamic Republic, Khamenei also earned the support of conservative clerics who controlled most of Iran's governmental institutions.

RAFSANJANI

Winning the presidential election with 95% of the votes after Khamenei's rise to the post of Supreme Leader was **Akbar Hashemi Rafsanjani**. Rafsanjani, who holds the Shi'ite clerical title of **Hojjat ol-Islam** (a slightly lower ranking than Ayatollah), had been an active participant in the Islamic Revolution. In the 1980s, then-speaker of the parliament Rafsanjani helped negotiate the secret arms-for-hostages deal with American President **Ronald Reagan** and played a key role in ending the Iran-Iraq war in 1988.

As president, Rafsanjani promoted friendly relations with the West and gradually opened the country to foreign investment. He also tried to move Iran towards a free market economy from a state-controlled system.

---

[84] Khomeini claimed the *faqih* could even supersede *shari'a* (Islamic) law if necessary.
[85] Montazeri claimed that the Supreme Religious Guide (or leader) was neither all-powerful nor infallible.

Rafsanjani was reelected for a second term in 1993 but by law, was barred from serving a third, consecutive term. He was succeeded in 1997 by Hojjat ol-Islam **Seyyed Muhammad Khatami**

KHATAMI

The landslide victory of reformist Khatami (who received nearly 69% of the votes) over the clerics' preferred candidate, **Nategh-Nouri,** (who won only 25% of the votes) in the 1997 presidential elections exposed widespread discontent over the status-quo. Unemployment had reached 20% in Iran, inflation had risen to 25% and per-capita income had dropped to an average of $800 per year from $1200 in 1979. Young people, who made up more than 65% of the country's population and by age 16 were allowed to vote, were frustrated by restrictions imposed by the conservative clerics in power. Women were fed-up with their lack of rights and the country's strict Islamic dress codes.[86]

The election of Khatami was a blow to conservative clerics and signaled what some called a "second revolution."

Khatami's campaign promoted the rule of law, democracy and greater rights for women. As Iran's first reformist president he set out to curb corruption, ease religious restrictions and allow a measure of free speech by giving the media more freedom. Dozens of papers emerged as a result and news coverage improved.

Khatami also mended fences with West European countries by visiting Italy and France and by declaring the Salman Rushdie issue "completely finished" – though he didn't have the religious authority to revoke Khomeini's *fatwa* against the British author. Britain reopened its embassy in Tehran soon after.

Despite Khatami's popularity and his democratic, reformist vision, though, he was powerless against the hard-line Islamists in the Iranian government who still controlled the Guardian Council, the judiciary and other powerful institutions and spiritual leader, **Khamenei**, who controlled the military, and held ultimate authority. Under their orders, more than 100 liberal publications were shut down, dozens of pro-reform activists and writers were detained and much of Khatami's reform legislation was blocked.

In 2001 Khatami again won reelection in a landslide victory but, by this point, many of his early supporters had become disillusioned by what they perceived as a very slow pace of reform and stayed home during the elections.[87] Khatami's second and last term ended in 2005.

---

[86] In keeping with Islamic values, women were required to cover their hair entirely and wear long, loose clothing to hide the shape of their bodies. Morality police and pious volunteers were dispatched around the country to enforce the dress code. Violators could be fined, imprisoned or even flogged.

[87] About 1 million voters did not vote in the 2001 election.

PRESIDENTIAL ELECTIONS 2005

The presidential run-off election of June 2005 pitted veteran politician **Rafsanjani** (Iran's president from 1989-1997) against the mayor of Tehran, **Mahmoud Ahmadinejad**. During his campaign, comparatively moderate and liberal Rafsanjani called for improved ties with the West. Ahmadinejad, in contrast, rejected Western "decadence" and intended to create a "modern, advanced and Islamic" role model for the world.

Rafsanjani, reportedly worth millions of dollars, was the frontrunner among Iran's progressive, affluent voters but **Ahmadinejad** had won the hearts of the country's poorer classes because of his modest and pious lifestyle and his campaign promises to tackle corruption, redistribute the country's oil wealth and provide monthly stipends to all citizens.

AHMADINEJAD

Before serving as Tehran's mayor from 2003-2005, Ahmadinejad was a great supporter of the Islamic Revolution and headed a hard-line student group while he was studying engineering. Several of the 52 hostages held at the American Embassy in 1979 claimed that he was one of their captors though the charges were fervently denied by Iranians who participated in the hostage crisis. During the Iran-Iraq war, Ahmadinejad joined the Islamic Revolutionary Guards Corps where he engaged in covert operations in the city of Kirkuk, Iraq. In 1993, Ahmadinejad served as the cultural advisor to then Ministry of Cultural and Higher Education and was appointed governor general of the newly established northwestern province of Adebil.

As mayor of Tehran, he aimed to reverse many of the reforms enacted by previous mayors, for example: shutting down fast-food restaurants, purportedly suggesting separate elevators for men and women in municipal buildings, requiring male employees to have beards and wear long sleeves and converting cultural centers into prayer halls, causing some to fear that he would enact conservative legislation throughout Iran during his rule.

In the first few months of his presidency, authorities banned imported films promoting secularism, feminism, violence and other un-Islamic behavior (foreign films with objectionable sexual content or scantily-clad women were already censored). Ahmadinejad also purged moderate diplomats from Tehran's embassies and barred all Western music from state radio and TV stations.

True to his populist platform, Ahmadinejad's government also blocked efforts to raise the highly subsidized price of gasoline, distributed rations of oil rice and sugar to the poor and increased government stipends given yearly to more than 1 million families through the Imam Khomeini Charity foundation.

Ahmadinejad provoked great indignation internationally when he suggested that the holocaust was a myth and that the state of Israel should be "wiped off the face of the earth." The President also aroused concern when he described Iran's nuclear program as a "flood which cannot be stopped by a matchstick" — although he maintained that the country was only pursuing nuclear technology for peaceful purposes.

Since formally, the president doesn't have the authority to shape the country's nuclear policy or foreign affairs, his comments were perceived as simply rhetorical.

The real power in Iran still resides with Supreme Leader Ayatollah Ali Khamenei who has remained close to the country's centrists led by Akbar Hashemi Rafsanjani.[88] While the hardliners believe confrontation with the west could help regenerate a sense of national purpose, the moderates recognize the high cost of international isolation and possibly, military confrontation.

---

[88] Khamenei enhanced the power of the Expediency Council and its Chairman, Rafsanjani, to oversee Ahmadinejad's government in October 2005. Ahmadinejad's nominees for the position of Oil Minister were also rejected by lawmakers upsetting the President's promise to purge a ministry he argues is controlled by a "mafia" and redistribute oil revenues among the poor.

ISLAM IN A NUTSHELL

According to Muslims, in A.D. 570[89] a prophet, **Muhammad** (also spelled Mohammed), was born in the city of Mecca in present-day Saudi Arabia. For the first 35 years of his life, Muhammad lived a quiet existence living with his wife, **Khadija**, their children (including a daughter **Fatima**) and his cousin **Ali** and spent his days tending to the family's caravan trade. One evening while he was meditating in a cave, he was visited by the angel **Gabriel** who brought the first of several messages from God (**Allah**) that would later be compiled into the **Quran**, Islam's holy book.[90]

The Prophet soon began to attract followers as he recounted Allah's messages to those who would listen. His growing popularity, though, caused concern among the powerful pagan families of Mecca.

The Meccan families persecuted and intimidated the small band of **Muslims** (or those who "submit" to God as they called themselves) until God instructed them to relocate to the city of **Yathrib** (later called **Medina**) in western Arabia. The date of the journey, called the *hijra*,[91] (migration) on July 16, 622 was later proclaimed the start of the Muslim era.[92]

During their time in Medina, the Muslims grew in strength and numbers until, eight years after their exile, Muhammad returned to Mecca with 10,000 Muslims and victoriously retook the city.

Caliphs

Two years later (632), Muhammad died and his companion, **Abu Bakr**, was named the leader or **Caliph** of the Muslim community by a committee of prominent men.

The election of **Abu Bakr** over Muhammad's cousin and son-in-law **Ali** (who had since married Muhammad's daughter **Fatima**), was protested by a small group of people who believed that Prophet Muhammad's successor should be a blood relative.

Abu Bakr was succeeded in 634 by **Umar ibn al Khattab** under whose leadership Islam spread to Palestine (Israel), Syria, Egypt and present-day Iraq.

When Umar was killed, an election committee selected **Uthman ibn Affan** to succeed him -- to the consternation of Ali's supporters.

---

[89] The actual year of Muhammad's birth is debated.

[90] Muhammad continued to receive messages from God over a 23-year period ending in 632, the year of his death.

[91] *Hijra* or *Hegira* means breaking off relations, abandoning one's tribe, for example, by migrating.

[92] Dated A.H. for *annus hegirae*. The year A.D. 623, for example, would be A.H. 1 according to the Muslim calendar and the year 2006 would be A.H. 1427. Unlike the Gregorian calendar (used throughout most of the world) the Muslim calendar follows the cycle of the moon rather than the sun. Islamic holidays, therefore, will land on different days each year in the West.

Uthman was murdered in A.D. 656 and the election committee finally chose Ali to succeed him. Ali's election was celebrated by his supporters who came to be known as the **Shi'at Ali**, the partisans of Ali or **Shi'as** but he was challenged by rival **Muawiyah I** from the **Umayyad** clan.

After Ali was assassinated in 661, **Muawiyah** was declared Caliph beginning the **Umayyad dynasty** and appointed his son, **Yazid**, to succeed him. But Ali's youngest son, **Husayn**, (his eldest son, **Hasan** had died after abdicating the throne to avoid a civil war) refused to pay homage to the new leader and, instead, led the Shi'as[93] in a revolt.

The small band of Shi'as, including women and children, marched to the city of **Karbala** (also spelled, "Kerbala," in present-day Iraq) where they were surrounded by 1000s of Yazid's troops. The **Umayyad** soldiers tortured and slaughtered the members of Husayn's party and paraded the heads of 72 of their victims (including the decapitated head of the Prophet's grandson, **Husayn**) through the town.

The massacre and martyrdom of Husayn took place on the 10th day of the month of **Muharram**, the day of **Ashura** ("tenth" in Arabic), and is commemorated yearly -- often by self-flogging in sympathy and as in symbolic self-punishment for not having come to Husayn's defense at Karbala.

The Shia's from that point on recognized a separate line of spiritual guides (called "**Imams**") beginning with Prophet Muhammad's cousin and son-in-law **Ali**, Ali's sons, **Hasan** and **Husayn** and continuing with their descendants.

Twelvers (Ithna-Ashara)

Most Iranian Shi'as recognize a succession of **twelve** descendants (hence the name "Twelvers") and believe that the twelfth descendant was placed in hiding (or "**occultation**") at the age of 5 to protect him from the enemies of Shi'ism.[94] The last Imam is expected to return as the **Mahdi** or Messiah before the Day of Judgment (the end of times) and establish justice and preach throughout the world by establishing Islam as a global religion.

12 Imams
Ali ibn Abu Talib (600-661)
Hasan ibn[123] Ali (625-669)
Husayn ibn Ali (626-680)
Ali Zayn al Abidin (658-713)
Muhammad al Baqir (676-743)
Jafar as Sadiq (703-765)
Musa al Kazim (745-799)
Ali ar Rida (765-818)
Muhammad at Taqi (810-835)
Ali al Hadi (827-868)
Hasan al Askari (846-874)
Muhammad al Mahdi (868- ?)

123 "Ibn" and "bin" both mean "the son of..." hence, Hasan, "son of" Ali.

Differences between Sunni and Shi'a Islam

Today about 85-90% of Muslims worldwide follow Sunni Islamic traditions and 10-15% of all Muslims are Shi'as. Both Sunnis and Shi'as observe the five basic tenets of Islam[95] but differ slightly in their religious prac-

---

93 Most of the Shi'as at that time lived in present-day southern Iraq.

94 Sunni Caliphs kept the Shi'a politically weak through persecution and by threatening the lives of their religious leaders. Hence, no Imams ever ruled politically.

95 Five main pillars of Islam: declaration of faith, prayer, alms to the poor, fasting (during the month of Ramadan) and pilgrimage to Mecca.

tices and beliefs. Only Shi'as commemorate the martyrdom of **Husayn**[96] and make regular pilgrimages to the holy Shi'a cities of **Karbala**[97] (where Husayn was killed) and **Najaf** (where the first "Imam," **Ali**, is entombed) in Iraq. Unlike Sunnis, Shi'as are also inclined to revere clerics as spiritual guides. While both Sunnis and Shi'as venerate and study the **Quran** as the word of God (Allah) spoken to Prophet **Muhammad** through the angel **Gabriel**, the two groups have different views on the authenticity of books written about Muhammad's life and teachings (collectively called the **Hadith**).

Islam in Iran
The Arab Muslims took control of Ctesiphon, capital city of the Zoroastrian-practicing **Sassanids**, in 637, five years after Muhammad's death, and won their ultimate victory over the Sassanids in 642. But the region was slow to convert to Islam and only the elite adopted the Arabic language[98] while the masses continued to speak Persian.

Non-Muslims in the growing Islamic Empire were permitted to practice their own religions as long as they paid a poll-tax (called a *jizya*) to their Islamic overlords. Initially, there was no serious attempt at mass conversion to Islam in the Persian areas.[99]

Eventually the majority of the population converted to Islam.

Safavids (1501-1736)
Ali's son, Husayn, was living in Mecca, Arabia when he was asked to lead the Shi'as in revolt against the rule of Muawiya's son, Yazid I. At that time, most Shi'a Muslims lived in the southern portion of present-day Iraq while the Muslims of Iran observed Sunni Islam.

That changed in the 16th century when the Safavids, led by **Ismail**, swept through Iran.

The Safavids began as a Sufi order (Sufism is a mystical branch of Sunni Islam) from Azerbaijan. They converted to Shi'ism by the 15th century and adopted a militant character forcing those they conquered to convert to Shi'a Islam.

In 1494 the Safavids were headed by **Ismail**, a young Safavid master who claimed to be a representative of the **hidden Imam** (he later claimed to be the last Imam himself). By 1512 the Safavids had conquered all of Iran and parts of Iraq (including Baghdad, Karbala and Najaf), implemented the use of Azeri in the courts and forced the population to convert to Shi'ism. The conversion was very successful. Today, Shi'a Islam is still the official state religion practiced by about 90% of Iran's population.

---

[96] Some Sunnis also recognize Ashura as the day Noah left the Ark, the day Muhammad arrived in Yathrib (Medina) and other incidents and consider the martyrdom of Husayn at the hands of the infidel Yazid as an unfortunate and significant historical event.

[97] Some Shi'as consider the city of Karbala a bridge to Paradise. For that reason, many Shi'as wish to have their bodies transported to the city for burial.

[98] Arabic became the official language of the court in 969.

[99] The Arabs initially believed Islam was exclusively an Arab religion (not Persian) and relied on income from the *jizya* (the tax collected from non-Muslims) to maintain the empire.

PATH TO BECOMING AN AYATOLLAH

Unlike Sunni Muslims, Shi'ite clerics are organized in a hierarchical structure which dates back to the establishment of Shi'ism as the state religion by the Safavids in the 16th century.

Advancement up the ranks of the clergy requires years of extensive theological education and the accumulation of a large following.

Future *mullahs* (clerics) begin by entering theological colleges (the most important are in the cities of Qom, Najaf [Iraq] and Mashhad) as **talib ilm** (students). For the first seven years, they study the Quran and other Islamic texts, take classes in Arabic (the language of the Quran) and learn about the lives of religious figures. At the intermediate level they study philosophy, science, literature and the works of great theologians (this takes another eight years). Once they graduate from the religious seminary, they will become **Mujtahid** and will be qualified to interpret Islamic texts for the people. At any point in their studies, students may go on to become local *mullahs* in a village (where they will guide their followers in day-to-day Islamic life and answer spiritual questions) or teach in one of the seminaries under the guidance of a higher-ranking cleric.

Further advancement is based on the size of the *Mujtahid's* following, publications of books he writes on religious topics and his insightful interpretations of Islamic texts. Once the cleric has gathered a large group of followers and earned the respect of his peers, he may be considered an **ayatollah**.

Grand Ayatollah (Ayatollah al-uzma)[a]
"Greatest sign of God"
Very few Grand Ayatollahs exist at any one time in the world.

Ayatollah
"Sign of God"
At this point, *mullahs* are expected to write lengthy dissertations on Islamic topics.

Hojat (Hojjat) al Islam
"Authority on Islam" or "Proof of Islam"

Mubellegh al risala
"Carrier of the message"

Mujtahid
One who has graduated from a religious seminary
One qualified to interpret Islam for the public

Talib ilm
Students
The "Taliban" in Afghanistan were so-named because they were students from Islamic schools (*madrassahs*) in Pakistan.

[a] This rank is a relatively recent creation used to distinguish the very top ayatollahs from the growing pool of clerics who had reached that level.

SHI'ITE GLOSSARY

Imam

The Arabic word "*imam*" means leader (e.g. the ruler of a country) but its meaning is slightly different in Islamic tradition. For Sunni Muslims, "imam" (spelled with a lower-case i) refers to any pious Muslim who leads the Friday prayer. To the Shi'as, the term "Imam" (upper case) is reserved for Prophet Muhammad's successors beginning with Ali, his sons Hasan and Husayn, and their descendants. Twelver Shi'as believe Muhammad was succeeded by 12 Imams — the last one still living in hiding or "occultation" until Judgment Day.

Mullah

Mullahs are Islamic clergy who have studied the Quran (Islam's holy book) and the Hadith (accounts of the life of Prophet Muhammad) and are considered experts on religious matters. Those who don black turbans are "*sayids*" or descendants of Muhammad. In Iran, *mullahs* were often related or connected to wealthy bazaar merchants or landowning families. Devout Shi'a Muslims generally give alms (an Islamic obligation) to local *mullahs,* to be redistributed to the poor.

Marja at-taqlid

Or "source of emulation." Shi'ite faithful traditionally choose a pious, knowledgeable cleric to be their spiritual guide and a source of emulation (imitation). Followers pay up to 1/5th of their income to their *Marja* as alms to be redistributed to the needy.

Vali-ye Faqih

A *faqih* is an Islamic jurist and *vali-ye faqih* means "guardian Islamic jurist"- an Islamic legal expert who exercises worldly power.
In his book, the *Velayat-e faqih* ("Guardianship of the Islamic Jurists") Khomeini states that all laws in an Islamic society should be based on the laws of Islam and that all activities should be governed by clerics well-versed in Islamic law. He believed that the leader of an Islamic Republic should be an Islamic Jurist *(faqih)* selected by an esteemed group of clerics (in Iran, the *Assembly of Experts*) to serve as "Supreme Leader" for life.

ZOROASTRIANISM[100]

Achaemenid Emperor **Cyrus the Great** is esteemed in Jewish literature and the Bible as the benevolent Persian king who released the Jews from 70 years of captivity in Babylon and helped them rebuild their Holy Temple in Jerusalem. In Persian history, he is celebrated as the founder of the Persian Empire by uniting the **Medes** and **Persians** and the ruler over the Greatest Empire ever seen. To the Zoroastrians, he is admired for his tolerance and generosity as demonstrated in his **Charter of Human Rights**[101] (the first of its kind) and acclaimed, especially, for being a fellow **Zoroastrian**.

Zarathustra (also known as **Zarathushtra** or **Zoroaster**)
The year, or even century, of **Zarathustra's** birth has been estimated from 3000 to 600 years before the birth of Christ making him, perhaps, the first person to worship one God whom he called **Ahura Mazda**.

According to Zoroastrians, **Ahura Mazda** (translated as the Lord or God [*Ahura*] of Wisdom [*Mazda*]) created the universe and infused life into all living things. Since the all-knowing, all-powerful, omnipresent, loving divinity has no form or color, his presence is symbolized by light and fire and Zoroastrians worldwide build **fire temples** to honor his radiant presence.

Gathas
In the course of his lifetime, Zarathustra is believed to have conversed with Ahura Mazda and compiled the dialogues written as poems or songs (so that they could be more easily memorized) into a body of work called the **Gathas**. The 17 orally-transmitted Gathas were written down in the **Parthian** and **Sassanian** periods of Persian history and incorporated into a larger book of prayers collectively known as the **Avesta.**

Good Thought, Good Words, Good Deeds
The Zoroastrian mantra, "Good Thoughts, Good Words, Good Deeds" is applied to every aspect of a believer's life. Zoroastrians are encouraged to aspire to a state of "perfection," or *Haurvatat,* and "immortality," or *Ameretat*, by observing and emulating the god-like attributes of *Vohu Mano* ("good thought") *Asha* ("truth and righteousness"), **Aramaiti** ("good acts"), **Vohu Khshathra** ("good rule").

Zoroastrianism in Iran
By the time **Cyrus the Great** founded the Persian Empire in 559 B.C. Zoroastrianism had spread all over the Iranian Plateau. Cyrus's tolerance for other religions within his empire reflected Zoroastrian ideals of tolerance and equality. The religion was also observed by **Darius the Great** and other Achaemenid rulers.

---

[100] For more on Zoroastrianism please visit www.enisen.com.

[101] Cyrus's declaration of human rights is preserved on a clay barrel, called the Cyrus Cylinder, and was translated by the United Nations in 1971 into all official languages. See www.enisen.com for a complete translation.

But many of the sacred texts were lost when **Alexander the Great** overthrew the Achaemenian Empire in 330 B.C., allowing his armies to pillage the Achaemenian religious capital of **Persepolis**.

The religion reemerged under the **Parthians** who had come to power in 247 B.C. and ruled over Persia when Jesus of Nazareth preached in Palestine. Some historians have theorized that the Three Wise Men who were believed to have visited Jesus' parents, Mary and Joseph, when he was born (the "Magi" in early Greek) were, in fact, Zoroastrians.

The **Sassanians**, who succeeded the **Parthians** in A.D. 228, formally deemed Zoroastrianism the state religion and aggressively promoted the religion. Unlike their predecessors, the Sassanians persecuted Christians and other religious minorities if they didn't convert and turned their places of worship into fire temples.

Zoroastrianism had spread as far as northern China by the time the Arab Muslims conquered Iran in A.D. 652 and mass conversions to Islam (by force, concession and choice) effectively rendered Zoroastrianism a minority religion itself.

To escape persecution, thousands of Zoroastrians fled to India in the 10th century where they were offered refuge by a Hindu king on the condition that they abstain from missionary activity and marry only within their community. The Indian Zoroastrians, who came to be known as the **Parsis**, maintain a thriving community.

The Zoroastrians who remained in Iran were tolerated as religious minorities until the Qajar era, when persecution and prejudice again resulted in the emigration of several thousand Zoroastrians to British-ruled India and other locations.

The status of Zoroastrians improved again under the Pahlavis and many Zoroastrians moved from the desert cities of **Yazd** and **Kerman** (where many had fled during the Mongol invasion in the 14th century) to **Tehran**.

Under the Islamic Constitution of 1979, the Zoroastrians are recognized as official religious minorities and permitted to elect one representative to the Majlis. They may also seek employment in the government.

Fravahar
(Zoroastrian symbol)

45

IRAN'S GOVERNMENT

CONSTITUTION[102]

In the last days of March 1979, a national referendum was held to determine the type of government to be established in post-Shah Iran. It was reported that a whopping 98% of the population voted in favor of an Islamic republic (the only choice on the ballot). Hence, on April 1, 1979, Ayatollah Khomeini established the **Islamic Republic of Iran**.

A few months later (August 1979), a 73-member **Assembly of Experts** was convened to draft a constitution[103] that would reflect Iran's new Islamic character as codified in Ayatollah Khomeini's work, the **Velayat-e Faqih** or "Government of the Islamic Jurists." According to Khomeini there should be no distinction between religion and government in an Islamic state and the only legitimate rulers would be the clergy.

The constitution was completed on November 15 and approved in another national referendum on December 2 and 3, 1979.

Preamble
"… In the view of Islam, government does not derive from the interests of a class, nor does it serve the domination of an individual or a group. Rather, it represents the fulfillment of the political ideal of a people who bear a common faith and common outlook, taking an organized form in order to initiate the process of intellectual and ideological evolution toward the final goal, i.e., movement towards Allah."

Highlights
Regarding the Media:
"The mass media must serve the diffusion of Islamic culture in pursuit of the evolutionary course of the Islamic Revolution."

Article 2 (Foundational Principles)
"The Islamic Republic is a system based on belief in:
    One God, Divine revelation
    The return to God in the Hereafter
    The justice of God in creation and legislation
    Continuous leadership and perpetual guidance and its fundamental
        role in ensuring the uninterrupted process of the revolution of Islam
    The exalted dignity and value of man, and his freedom coupled with
        responsibility before God
    Continuous leadership of the holy persons, possessing necessary quali-
        fications, exercised on the basis of the Koran and the Sunnah
    Sciences and arts, Negation of all forms of oppression"

---

[102] See www.enisen.com for a complete transcript of Iran's constitution.

[103] An early draft drawn up by the Provisional Government was based on Iran's 1906 Constitution calling for a strong presidency and with no mention of the position of *Faqih* (Islamic jurist). Protests by the more conservative elements within the *ulema* (Islamic clergy) prompted Khomeini to empower an elected Assembly of Experts to amend and redraft the earlier constitution.

Article 3 (State Goals)
(A selection)
"Elimination of imperialism and the prevention of foreign influence"
"Elimination of all forms of despotism and autocracy"
"Legal protection for all, as well as the equality of all before the law"
"The expansion and strengthening of Islamic brotherhood and public cooperation"
"Fraternal commitment to all Muslims, and unsparing support to the freedom fighters of the world."

Article 4 (Islamic Principle)
"All civil, penal, financial, economic, administrative, cultural, military, political and other laws and regulations must be based on Islamic criteria."

Article 5 (Office of Religious Leader)
"During the occultation of the Walki al-'Asr[104] (may God hasten his reappearance), the leadership of the Ummah devolve upon the just and pious person, who is fully aware of the circumstances of his age, is courageous, resourceful, and possessed of administrative ability, and who will assume the responsibilities of this office in accordance with Article 107."

Article 12 (Official Religion)
"The official religion of Iran is Islam and the Twelver Ja'fari school."

Article 13 (Recognized Religious Minorities)
"Zoroastrian, Jewish and Christian Iranians are the only recognized religious minorities who, within the limits of the law, are free to perform their religious rites and ceremonies and to act according to their own canon in matters of personal affairs and religious education."

Article 15 (Official Language)
"The official language is Persian."

Article 16 (Arabic Language)
"Since the language of the Koran and Islamic texts and teachings is Arabic, and since Persian literature is thoroughly permeated by this language, it must be taught after elementary level, in all classes of secondary school and in all areas of study."

"Article 17 (Official Calendar)
The Official Calendar of the country takes as its point of departure the migration of the Prophet of Islam – God's peace and blessings upon him and his Family. Both the solar and lunar Islamic calendars are recognized, but government offices will function according to the solar calendar. The official weekly holiday is Friday."

---

[104] Article 4 refers to the Mahdi, the last of the twelve Imams who, Shi'a Muslims believe, went into hiding ("occultation") at age 5 in A.D. 873. The Mahdi is expected to reappear in the last days of the earth and establish peace, justice and truth throughout the world by establishing Islam as a global religion. According to Iran's constitution, power over the *Ummah* (Islamic community) will rest with the Supreme Leader, whose responsibilities are outlined in Article 107 of the constitution, until the Mahdi returns. Sunni Muslims believe the Mahdi has not yet been born.

Articles regarding civil rights (27, 32, 33,34,35,36,37,38, 39)

"Public gatherings and marches may be freely held, provided arms are not carried and that they are not detrimental to the fundamental principles of Islam. No one may be arrested except by the order and in accordance with the procedure laid down by law. Charges must be explained to the accused in writing. It is the indisputable right of every citizen to seek justice by recourse to competent courts. Both parties to a lawsuit have the right in all courts of law to select an attorney, and if they are able to do so, arrangements must be made to provide them with legal counsel. Innocence is to be presumed. All forms of torture for the purpose of extracting confession or acquiring information are forbidden."

Article 56 (Divine Right of Sovereignty)

"Absolute sovereignty over the world and man belongs to God and it is He who has made man master of his own social destiny."

***

SUPREME LEADER (*Faqih*)

The Supreme Leader is the most important representative of Islamic authority and the Head of State. The position was filled by **Ayatollah Khomeini** until his death in 1989. In order to accommodate Khomeini's successor, **Ali Khameini** (who had only reached the rank of **Hojat al Islam** by the time of Khomeini's death),[105] the constitution was amended to allow the post to be held by a lower-ranking theologian. The powers of the Supreme Leader were also expanded.

Theoretically, the Supreme Leader is selected by the populace. In truth, he is elected by an **Assembly of Experts** whose members are elected by public vote. The Supreme Leader serves for life.[106]

The Supreme Leader controls the armed forces and the internal security forces and has the sole power to declare war. He also has the power to appoint and dismiss the leaders of the judiciary, half the members of the Council of Guardians and the head of the state radio and television networks. He can also dismiss the president of the Republic if he is found guilty of violating his constitutional duties by the Supreme Court or if he is found incompetent by the **Majles** (the legislature).

The Supreme Leader must be a member of the Shi'a clergy and exhibit extensive Islamic scholarship.

---

[105] **Ayatollah Ali Khamenei** achieved his Constitutional position of *faqih* as a result of his political activism rather than because of his scholarship and therefore is held in contempt by many of the more senior Shi'ite Islamic scholars. Indeed, Khamenei was only promoted from *hojat al Islam* to *ayatollah* by the Iranian government on the eve of his taking office as *faqih*. Khamenei had never written any major Islamic tracts or developed a strong student following while teaching at an Islamic seminary. In contrast, Khamenei's rival, **Ayatollah Ali Montazeri**, had high religious credentials.

[106] Only the Assembly of Experts can depose the Supreme Leader.

PRESIDENT

Although the president is second in command after the Supreme Leader, his power is very limited (as was exhibited under the rule of reformist President Khatami). All candidates for the presidency must be approved by the **Council of Guardians** before they can run for office and must believe in the official *madhhab* (Islamic school of thought) of the country — that is, they must be Twelver Shi'a Muslims. They also must be of Iranian origin and nationality.

The president is elected directly by the people for a 4-year term and can serve a maximum of two terms. His primary job is to make sure that the constitution is faithfully observed and executed. He signs and supervises the implementation of laws passed by the Majles, signs treaties, receives foreign ambassadors and endorses Iranian ambassadors. The president also administers the country's budget.

After the post of prime minister was eliminated in 1989 the president also took on the powers that were previously given to the prime minister.

MAJLES or ISLAMIC CONSULTATIVE ASSEMBLY (Parliament)

In 1906, the Shah bowed to popular pressure and agreed to draft a constitution and establish a representative legislative body, the Majles. Today, the Majles consists of 290 members who are elected directly by the people in a secret ballot for 4-year terms. Like the president, all candidates must first be approved by the Council of Guardians.

Among the members are representatives of the Zoroastrians (1), Jews (1), Armenian Christians (2), Assyrians and Chaldean Christians (1 member representing both groups).

The Majles is responsible for drafting legislation, ratifying international treaties, and approving the country's budget – all actions are reviewed by the Council of Guardians.

COUNCIL OF GUARDIANS (Guardian Council of the Constitution)

The Council of Guardians is the highest and most powerful institution in the government and is currently dominated by conservatives. The office is made up of six religious men chosen by the Supreme Leader and six lawyers (also Islamic scholars) specializing in different areas of law elected by the judiciary and approved by the Majles. All serve six-year terms.

Members of the council review all laws to determine whether they are in line with the constitution and *sharia* (Islamic law). If they are found to be against Islam or Iran's constitution, the laws are vetoed.[107] Council members also examine presidential and parliamentary candidates before they can run for a seat.[108]

---

[107] This gives the conservative Council the power to veto reformist legislation.

[108] In the 2004 parliamentary election, for example, the Council disqualified more than 2000 pro-reform and independent candidates. In 2005, all but a handful of the more than 1000 presidential candidates were disqualified (few reformers were permitted to run).

IRAN'S NUCLEAR PROGRAM

Iran's nuclear program began in the late 1950s under Mohammed Reza Shah when Iran was still on good terms with the United States. At the time, the United States was offering technical assistance and supplies to friendly nations that were interested in producing nuclear energy – a product of Eisenhower's **Atoms for Peace** program.[109]

With U.S. encouragement, the Shah ordered the establishment of a nuclear research center at Tehran University in 1959 and soon after that, the U.S. supplied Iran with a research reactor and a "start-up source" of enriched uranium and plutonium. In 1968, Iran was also one of the first nations to sign the **Nuclear Non Proliferation Treaty (NPT**, ratified in 1970) which required countries with nuclear know-how to help non-nuclear states develop peaceful nuclear power in return for the promise that they would never develop nuclear weapons.

Although Iran in the 1970s had plenty of oil, the regime feared that the country's supply of oil reserves would be exhausted in about 30 years. To forestall any energy problems, the Shah planned to use Iran's oil money to build sufficient nuclear power plants to generate 23,000 megawatts of electricity by 1994.

For nearly a decade after signing the **NPT**, Iran received billions of dollars worth of nuclear supplies, equipment and technical support from France (who helped install reactors in the city of Bushehr), the United States, Britain, Germany, Denmark, South Africa and other nations.

However, all the nuclear power activity came to an abrupt halt in 1978.

Iran's nuclear program under Khomeini

From the beginning, Ayatollah Khomeini denounced all nuclear weapons as contrary to Islamic values.[110] As information began to emerge that Iraq was pursuing nuclear weapons, however, interest in the pursuit of nuclear energy began to pick up once again. This time, the Iranians turned to China, Pakistan and eventually Russia, which signed a nuclear technology cooperation agreement with Iran in 1990,[111] for their help developing nuclear energy.

With Russia's help, the Iranians worked to rebuild reactors at Bushehr (which had been bombed repeatedly by the Iraqis during the 1980-88 Iran-Iraq war) and took advantage of the expertise of the "father of the Pakistani nuclear program," **Dr. Abdul Qadeer Khan.**

---

[109] The escalating nuclear arms race between the U.S. and the USSR inspired U.S. President Eisenhower to seek a solution to the "atomic dilemma" by finding ways in which the "inventiveness of man would not be dedicated to his death, but consecrated in his life. Eisenhower's 1953 "Atoms for Peace" speech to the UN resulted in a number of peaceful atomic programs and prompted the U.S. to sign a civil nuclear cooperation agreement with Iran in 1957.

[110] Iran's current president Ahmadinejad and other Iranian leaders also made that claim.

[111] In 2005, Russia tried to break the impasse in talks between the United Nations and Iran over uranium enrichment (which is needed to complete the nuclear "fuel cycle" in order to produce energy and build bombs) by suggesting that Iran be allowed to conduct uranium enrichment in Russia.

Nuclear power or weapons?

Iran has repeatedly claimed that it is only interested in developing nuclear power and has no intention of building nuclear weapons. In August, 2005, Supreme Leader Ayatollah Ali Khamenei even issued a *fatwa* (a legal ruling by an Islamic cleric) forbidding the production, stockpiling and use of nuclear weapons.

Critics in the U.S. government, though, doubt this claim, contending that Iran has more than enough natural gas to make 500 megawatts of electricity each year. U.S. President **George W. Bush** and his supporters maintain that Iran's primary purpose for building nuclear reactors is to develop nuclear weapons.

Iranian officials have pointed out that under the terms of the **Non-Proliferation Treaty** or NPT (Article IV in particular), which Iran joined in 1974,[112] Iran has the legal right to develop its nuclear power program with help from other nuclear-powered nations.

As for America's claim that Iran has enough natural gas to produce all the electricity that the country needs, Iranians have calculated that the rate of Iran's demand for electricity has been growing at such a fast pace that the country will be forced to import oil by the year 2021 if it doesn't find an alternative source of energy – a disastrous fate for a country that obtains 80% of its export earnings from oil.[113] Although the start-up costs for building a nuclear power program are steep, relying on nuclear plants for Iran's power needs allows Iran to sell surplus oil that it currently burns to generate electricity.

Defense

Energy needs aside, there is no question that Iran would benefit from having a nuclear weapons arsenal for defensive purposes. In the 1980s, the threat of Iraq acquiring nuclear weapons was especially daunting, especially in light of the destruction Saddam Hussein caused in Iran by employing chemical weapons during the Iran-Iraq war. Iran is also surrounded by American allies with nuclear weapons of their own (Israel [allegedly], Pakistan and Russia).

National Pride

Some analysts claim that Iran is not an immediate nuclear threat[114] and that actual atomic warfare is unlikely since any country aggressive enough to use nuclear weapons against a rival is sure to be obliterated itself. Rather, the benefit to having a nuclear weapons arsenal is political and psychological.

For Iran, maintaining a healthy nuclear program would be a source of national pride exhibiting to the world that Iran is as advanced technologically as the other nuclear states and a regional force to be reckoned with.

---

[112] In February 2006, Iranian President Ahmadinejad threatened to withdraw from the NPT if international pressure increased over Iran's nuclear program. The North Koreans left the NPT in 2003 and have since produced enough fuel for six or more nuclear weapons

[113] About a quarter of the world's electricity is generated by nuclear power plants today and even countries that have their own gas reserves -- Russia, Great Britain and Canada, for example -- employ nuclear power.

[114] According to some predictions, Iran will not have weapons before 2008.

With nuclear weapons, Iran's prestige among Islamic countries would sky-rocket as it became the most powerful counterforce to Israel, currently the only country in the region believed to have nuclear weapons.

A nuclear weapons program could also be used as a bargaining chip against Iran's enemies and ultimately deter an American invasion.[115]

The controversy

According to the terms of the **Nuclear Non-Proliferation Treaty (NPT)**, signatories are required to notify the **IAEA**[116] whenever work is done in their nuclear facilities. For the last 18 years, though, Iran has pursued nuclear activities without consulting the organization. The Americans claim that Iran's concealment of its nuclear activity and its suspicious behavior with IAEA inspectors proves that the country has military intentions which would violate **NPT** terms. As punishment, U.S. officials worked to bring Iran in front of the UN Security Council to face possible sanctions.

Iranian officials said that the country was forced to seek expertise and materials secretly from black market sources because U.S. sanctions prevented them from openly acquiring what they needed on the international market.

Iran's clandestine nuclear activity was discovered in 2002 when a coalition of Iranian opposition groups based outside Iran called the **National Council of Resistance of Iran** (NCRI) and counting **Mujahedin-e Khalq Organization** or **MEK** among its members, disclosed that Iran had secretly built uranium-enrichment and Heavy Water Reactor plants in Iran. Although **MEK** has been known to have made exaggerated claims about Iran in the past, the information was investigated by authorities and confirmed. Iran had built a uranium enrichment plant in **Natanz** (which could be used to fuel power plants or nuclear bombs) and had begun construction on a "**Heavy Water Reactor**" in **Arak** (which could be used to produce weapons-grade plutonium or could have civilian uses.)[117] Both the facilities could be relatively quickly converted to produce material for making nuclear weapons. They could also be copied and built secretly elsewhere. But Iranians maintained that they were not interested in building weapons and that the facilities were perfectly in-line with NPT requirements.

The argument has been made that Iran doesn't need a uranium enrichment plant at all since Tehran has only one nuclear power station that requires lightly enriched uranium fuel and Russia has promised to supply Iran with all the

---

[115] Rhetoric about a possible U.S. invasion of Iran has only confirmed Iran's need for self-defense. Moreover, America's invasion of Iraq, a country that Iran was unable to defeat after eight years of warfare, has enhanced the belief that the only way a country can defend itself from a U.S. attack is by acquiring nuclear weapons.

[116] The **International Atomic Energy Agency** (IAEA) is a United Nations watchdog created in 1953 to promote the peaceful use of nuclear technology and inhibit its use for military purposes. The IAEA advises the Security Council when countries violate NPT agreements by using peaceful energy program to develop nuclear weapons.

[117] Hard Water Reactors (HWRs) are usually used to bypass uranium enrichment to produce plutonium which could be used for nuclear weapons. HWRs can also be used for medical and agricultural purposes, the process is identical.

enriched uranium it needs for the entire lifetime of the reactor.[118] The compromise was intended to prevent Iran from obtaining the technology needed for making nuclear weapons.

In 2003, IAEA inspectors also discovered traces of highly-enriched weapons-grade uranium at several once secret installations in Iran, including a former watch factory called the **Kalaye Electric Company**. It was later discovered that the suspicious uranium belonged to the previous owner of the reactors, Pakistan, further adding weight to Iran's claim that its nuclear program was unfairly scrutinized by the West.

In 2003, Britain, France and Germany (EU-3) attempted to mediate the problem diplomatically by offering Iran incentives if the country abandoned its uranium-enrichment program – which Iran agreed to do temporarily.[119] As negotiations proceeded, though, it became clear that the Europeans expected Iran to permanently cease enriching uranium while the Iranians expected to resume their activity when negotiations had ended. As negotiations dragged on without producing compelling economic incentives,[120] Iran became restless and finally decided to resume uranium reprocessing, despite Europe's threat to refer the country to the U.N. Security Council for possible sanctions if it did.

If Iran did successfully develop nuclear weapons, the balance of power in the Middle East would shift dramatically. What the West fears most is the threat that terrorists supported by Iran would get their hands on the weapons.

Shahab Missiles

Between 1988 and 1994, Iran began making Shahab-1 long-range missiles with help from North Korea. The Shahab-1 missile has a range of about 190 miles, enough to strike Baghdad during the Iran-Iraq war.

In July 2003, Iran added the Shahab-3 medium-range ballistic missile to its military arsenal. The Shahab-3 has a range of about 800 miles, which could easily reach Israel, and is fully capable of carrying nuclear warheads.

Dissident groups have claimed that Iran also has a Shahab 4 and is developing the missile to stages 5 and 6 with the help of Russia and in cooperation with North Korea. The Shahab-5 and 6 would have a 2,000-3,700 mile range, capable of hitting the eastern edge of the United States.

---

[118] President Ahmadinejad discounted offers from Europe and Russia to sell Iran enriched nuclear fuel for fear that Iran would become dependent on the selling country for maintenance of its nuclear powerplants. Comparing the offer to sales of aircraft he said "every country that sells aircraft to other countries is required to sell its spare parts as well. For 27 years you have refused to give us aircraft spare parts. How can we be sure that you will give us nuclear fuel?"

[119] In October 2003, Iran decided to voluntarily suspend all uranium enrichment and reprocessing activities as defined by the IAEA. The pledge was reaffirmed in Nobember 2004 "to build confidence." On September 2, 2005, Iran resumed uranium conversion at Esfahan and, on January 10, 2006, removed U.N. seals at Natanz uranium enrichment plant and resumed research on nuclear fuel.

[120] In return for dropping its uranium enrichment program, the Bush administration offered to end American opposition to Iran's application for membership in the World Trade Organization and a partial lifting of the ban on sales of spare parts for Iran's civilian aircraft.

BUILDING A NUCLEAR BOMB

Nuclear Fission

When atoms split into two roughly equal pieces— or undergo "**fission**" — they release a great deal of energy (called "**nuclear energy**") in the form of heat. In some cases, the atom fragments hit other atoms which then split themselves creating more heat. Under the right conditions, they will continue to split causing a self-sustaining **fission chain reaction** that will continue indefinitely releasing greater and greater amounts of energy and heat.

When the fission chain is controlled in a **nuclear reactor**, the energy can be converted into electricity (**nuclear power**). In a **nuclear weapon**, the chain reaction isn't controlled, causing horrible destruction.

In order to create nuclear fission, one must start with fissionable materials – specifically, **highly enriched uranium** or **plutonium**. Both can be used to create **nuclear energy** and **nuclear weapons**.

Uranium [121]

Uranium is a natural element found in a large variety of minerals and in seawater. But only a small percentage (7 of 1000 atoms) of naturally occurring uranium contains **uranium-235** – the ingredient needed to generate a **fission chain reaction** (the other 993 atoms are composed of **uranium-238**).

Countries that have nuclear programs usually try to mine their own supply of uranium so that they will not be dependent on other nations for their supply. Iran reportedly has opened as many as 10 uranium mines.

Once mined, the uranium ore, often still in rock form, is taken to a uranium mill where it is crushed and mixed with water and other particles until it becomes a compound called **yellow cake**. The yellow cake is then converted into **uranium hexafluoride** and then **enriched** to separate the **uranium-235** from the uranium-238. The extent of the enrichment is determined by the purpose of the uranium – greater **enrichment** produces a higher concentration of **uranium-235** (up to 90%, called "weapons-grade uranium")[122] which can be used to create nuclear weapons. Less enrichment is needed for peaceful, civilian, energy-producing purposes (called "**low-enriched uranium**" or **LEU**).

The entire process, from the preparation of uranium to the disposal of radioactive **spent fuel** (the leftover uranium-238) is called the **nuclear fuel cycle**. **Spent fuel** can also be stored or reprocessed to produce plutonium.

[121] "Uranium" was named after the planet Uranus. For many years it was used primarily to color ceramic glazes and as a tint for early photography. Its special radioactive quality (that is, its ability to undergo fission) wasn't discovered until 1866. Most nuclear power plants today use **enriched uranium**.

[122] Traces of **highly enriched uranium** found in **centrifuges** (equipment used to separate uranium-235 and uranium-238) led to suspicion that Iran was trying to produce weapons-grade uranium to be used in nuclear weapons. It was later discovered that the highly enriched uranium was in fact left over from the previous user of the equipment, Pakistan.

Plutonium[123]

Unlike uranium, plutonium doesn't occur naturally but is made from **spent fuel** from a nuclear reactor (uranium-238 converted into plutonium[124]). Although far smaller quantities of plutonium are needed to create power[125] and build a bomb,[126] it is much harder to work with and extremely dangerous to handle.

In order to dissolve and then separate the un-used uranium from plutonium, a process called **reprocessing** is applied. The separated plutonium is then fabricated into nuclear fuel or nuclear weapons. Like uranium, different degrees of pure plutonium are used for different purposes. "**Reactor-grade**" plutonium contains less than 80% plutonium-239 while "**weapons-grade plutonium**" will contain 80-93% pure plutonium-239. Although both can be used to make nuclear weapons, "weapons-grade plutonium" is preferred since it is less difficult to handle.

Reprocessing rather than disposing spent fuel allows poorer countries to extract all the energy they can from their uranium supply and reduces nuclear waste.[127] But countries with significant processing facilities (which can be small enough to be easily hidden) are usually aiming to produce nuclear weapons. Security analysts have always worried that states would pursue "civilian" reprocessing programs and then convert them to weapons with little notice.

Nuclear power plant and nuclear weapons

Both peaceful power reactors and those used to produce nuclear weapons produce plutonium. But civilian electrical power reactors are typically much larger than military production reactors and produce many times more plutonium than military reactors.

---

[123] The name "plutonium" comes from the planet Pluto.

[124] Plutonium-239 is produced when the most common isotope of uranium 238 absorbs neutrons and then quickly decays to plutonium. "Reactor-grade" plutonium consists of less than 80% plutonium-239.

[125] Plutonium has been used to power scientific equipment in lunar exploration and implanted heart pacemakers. Plutonium is tens of thousands of times more radioactive than uranium.

[126] Plutonium is often preferred to enriched uranium for compact warheads on missiles because it takes a small amount to produce a significant blast.

[127] Arguments against the need for reprocessing spent fuel point to the fact that there is a glut in cheap uranium in the world and that plutonium-based "mixed-oxide" (MOX) fuel for power reactors is 6-10 times more expensive than comparable fuel.

NUCLEAR NON-PROLIFERATION TREATY (NPT)

The **Nuclear Non-Proliferation treaty**, signed by 189 countries, was put into effect in March 1970 to prevent the spread of nuclear weapons and weapons technology by fostering the peaceful uses of nuclear energy. According to the agreement, nations with nuclear know-how are required to dismantle their arsenals and help non-nuclear states develop power for peaceful purposes. In return, non-nuclear weapon states (non-NWS) vow never to develop nuclear weapons.

Despite the peaceful aim of the NPT, critics have complained that some of the nuclear nations are not living up to their side of the deal and other signatories are using their membership as a cover to create their own weapons program. Since there is no penalty for dropping out of the program, moreover, countries, such as North Korea, can pull out any time without repercussions (for example, to embark on a nuclear weapons program). Other countries — India, Pakistan and Israel, who all have nuclear weapons and are situated in volatile regions — have never joined the NPT, allowing them to develop and process nuclear weapons without legal obstacles.

Nuclear States: Only 5 NPT member countries are allowed to have nuclear weapons: the United States, the United Kingdom, France, Russia and China. These were the only countries possessing such weapons when the treaty was written and are also the five permanent members of the UN Security Council. All agree not to transfer nuclear weapons technology to other countries and the non–nuclear weapons countries agree not to develop nuclear weapons.

Article IV:

"Nothing in this Treaty shall be interpreted as affecting the inalienable right of all the Parties to the Treaty to develop research, production and use of nuclear energy for peaceful purposes without discrimination and in conformity with articles I and II of this Treaty." "All the Parties to the Treaty ... have the right to fully participate in the exchange of equipment, materials and scientific and technological information for the peaceful uses of nuclear energy."

Loophole: According to Article IV, member states are permitted to enrich uranium for fuel reasons. However, once uranium is enriched, it is only a small step away from developing nuclear warheads. This can be done in secret or by withdrawing from the NPT (like North Korea in 2003).

Article VI:

"Each of the Parties to the Treaty undertakes to pursue negotiations in good faith on effective measures relating to cessation of the nuclear arms race at an early date and to nuclear disarmament, and on a Treaty on general and complete disarmament under strict and effective international control."

Article X:

"Each Party has the right to withdraw from the Treaty if it decides that extraordinary events, related to the subject matter of the Treaty, have jeopardized the supreme interests of its country. It shall give notice of such withdrawal to all other Parties to the Treaty and to the United Nations Security Council three months in advance. Such notice shall include a statement of the extraordinary events it regards as having jeopardized its supreme interests."

THE POLITICS OF OIL

Iran, which is sitting on more than 9% of all the known oil in the world, exports about 3 million barrels of oil per day (its quota as set by **OPEC**) ranking it the fourth largest exporter of oil behind Saudi Arabia, Norway, and the United Kingdom.[128]

Today, more than 80% of Iran's income is earned by exporting its "black gold" accounting for about 40-50% of the government's budget.

Background

One of the first people to write about Iran's oil potential was a French geologist and mining engineer by the name of **Jacques de Morgan**. His paper on the study of crude oil deposits in Iran[129] was brought to the attention of **William Knox D'Arcy**, a wealthy Englishman who agreed to finance the exploration for oil in the Persian Empire.

In 1901, **D'Arcy** received a 60-year concession to drill in southern Persia from the Qajar Shah, **Mozafar'od-Din**. Seven years later, D'Arcy and his team struck oil in **Masjid-e Suleiman**.

To manage the oil, D'Arcy established the **Anglo-Persian Oil Company (APOC)** and began construction on a pipeline to take oil from Masjid-i-Suleiman to a refinery at **Abadan**, an island in the Persian Gulf. By that time, though, he had run low on funds and had to sell 97% of the company's shares to the Scottish **Burmah Oil Company** to keep the venture afloat.

WWI

In the early 20th century, the British government decided to fuel its Royal Navy warships with oil instead of coal and they became **Anglo-Persian Oil Company's** biggest buyers – so big, in fact, that the British government

---

OPEC

The **Organization of the Petroleum Exporting Countries (OPEC)** was formed in 1960 in Baghdad in response to the establishment of the American **Mandatory Oil Import Quota Program (MOIP)** which restricted the amount of crude oil that could be imported into the United States. The **MOIP** favored oil imports from Mexico and Canada at the expense of the Persian Gulf producerss, causing Middle East oil prices to drop.

The founding members of **OPEC** (Iraq, Iran, Kuwait, Saudi Arabia and Venezuela) — who were the source of over 80% of the world's crude oil exports — created the organization in order to restore higher oil prices by regulating the output of oil by OPEC member states. A smaller supply of oil would command higher prices and set quotas were implemented to prevent economic fluctuations and protect countries that were threatened by punitive international sanctions.

OPEC **quotas** are determined by the overall size of a country's oil reserves, the condition of its oil infrastructure, its capacity to produce and transport oil, demographic and economic considerations, the degree of the country's dependency on oil revenues and the demand of a specific country's oil.

---

[128] Iran is the second largest oil exporting member of OPEC.

[129] Titled "Note sur les Gites de Naphte de Kand-i-Shirin."

under Prime Minister **Winston Churchill** decided to safeguard its access to Persian oil by buying half the company in preparation for the looming war (World War I). By 1912, Britain owned 51% of the Anglo-Persian Oil Company and had appointed members to the company's board of directors to ensure that the British Navy received a constant supply of cheap oil.

Reza Shah and the Pahlevi Dynasty
In 1925, the last ruler of the Qajar dynasty was deposed and soon after, **Reza Khan Pahlevi** ascended the "Peacock Throne" to become Persia's new Shah.

The new Shah had a lot of ambitious plans for his country that required significant funding and he looked to the British-owned Anglo-Persian Oil Company as a source. When the British balked at the Shah's demand for a 25% share in APOC, the Shah deemed the D'Arcy concession invalid since it had been granted by Qajar leaders who were no longer in power. In retaliation, the British reduced output and, consequently, export earnings, and threatened war.

The matter was finally settled in 1933 – Persia got 20% of shares in the company, guaranteed annual payments and other awards and D'Arcy's concession was extended another 30 year. But relations between the Shah and the British government remained shaky from that point on contributing to Shah Reza Pahlevi's decision to befriend Germany. For the next few years, the Shah invited Germans, Italians and other foreign experts to provide the country with technical assistance.

World War II
As World War II approached, the demand for oil grew and the need to protect its source became even more critical. In order to make sure that Iranian oil didn't fall into enemy (German) hands, therefore, Britain and the Soviet Union asked the Shah to expel all German nationals from the country. When the Shah refused, the British and Soviets invaded Iran, arrested the Shah and forced him to abdicate. His son, **Reza Shah** – a supporter of the **Allied** forces of Britain, France, the Soviet Union and later the United States – was encouraged to take the throne in his place.

The foreign troops were withdrawn from Iran after World War II but the occupation and the growing demand for oil prompted Iran to reexamine its economic and political international relations.

Nationalization of Oil
By the mid 20th century Iran still controlled only 20% of its oil industry while most other oil-producing countries enjoyed 50/50 profit sharing agreements. For years the **Anglo-Iranian Oil Company** (renamed when "Persia" became "Iran" in 1935) had been bilking Iran by underreporting profits, refusing to pay taxes and charging exorbitant amounts for the maintenance of the pipelines. Iranians also were aware that Britain was making more money from taxing AIOC than Iran was making in royalties.

The discrepancy had become one of the most popular issues during the 1949 elections for the Majles (parliament) and steps were taken to renegotiate the terms of the AIOC as soon as the Majles was in session. At the head of the negotiating committee was **Dr. Mohammed Mossadegh**, a Majles member who founded and led the **National Front of Iran** (*Jebhe Melli*), an organization that aimed to end the exploitation of Iran's oil resources.

After some discussion, the Majles offered the British a 50/50 deal on the company. When that was rejected, the Majles voted on March 15, 1951 to take over complete control of the AIOC by nationalizing the oil industry.

The bill was expectedly upheld by **Mossadegh** who was overwhelming voted in by the Majles in April 1951 to replace **Ali Razmara** (who had been assassinated in early March) as Iran's prime minister. Soon after Mossadegh came to power, the **Anglo-Iranian Oil Company** was renamed the **National Iranian Oil Company** (NIOC) and put under Iran's control. The **Abadan** refinery (at the time the largest refinery in the world supplying 43% of Europe's oil) was taken over almost immediately.

Because of Mossadegh's great popularity, Reza Shah had little choice but to give his consent.

1951 Abadan Oil Crisis
The decision to nationalize Iran's oil occured at the height of the post-WWII Cold War between the United States and the Soviet Union and at a critical time for Europe.

The Soviets had made little secret about their designs on Iranian oil,[130] causing uneasiness in the United States, and World War II had shown just how vital oil had become in the pursuit of world power and how disastrous the lack of oil could be.

In 1941, the Japanese had invaded Indochina in order to get access to its oil and bombed Pearl Harbor to prevent American naval ships from intercepting the supply line of oil from the East Indies to Japan. Germany, which tried to produce synthetic oil from coal to make up for its lack of natural oil, had its eyes on the oil fields in the Caucasus and the Caspian Sea when Hitler invaded the Soviet Union – but was forced to retreat because the German military vehicles ran out of gas before they could reach Moscow.

Oil also proved critical to postwar recovery in Europe when, in 1946, a shortage of coal had caused a severe energy crisis. At the time, approximately half of Europe's petroleum came from U.S. companies. But that changed drastically when American consumption of oil began to outgrow its level of production. By 1951, about 80% of Europe's oil supply was expected to come from the Middle East – for the British that meant relying on the **Anglo-Iranian Oil Company** and Britain was not going

---

[130] Soviet oil production in 1945 was only 60% of that in 1941 because of serious damage to its refineries in Baku. The Soviets had hoped to bully Iran into giving them an oil concession after World War II by refusing to vacate the country along with its WWII allies. The incident (known as the Iranian Crisis of 1946) nearly set off a major East-West confrontation.

to give up control of the company without a fight.

To punish Iran for taking over **AIOC,** the British blocked all Iranian oil exports and threatened legal action against foreign companies that shipped "stolen oil" from Iran. The British also froze Iranian assets held in U.K banks and banned the export of goods to Iran. By acting forcefully (even at British expense), Britain hoped to discourage Egypt and other Middle East countries from following Iran's example -- for example by attempting to nationalize the Suez Canal.[131]

In order to prevent Iran from falling into Soviet hands, the United States acted as mediator by discouraging Iran from taking military action and trying to encourage Mossadegh to compromise by allowing a consortium of companies from various countries to jointly process, sell and transport Iranian oil at much favorable financial terms.

Iranian oil production had come to a near standstill after nationalization and exports had dwindled due to the embargo[132] wreaking havoc on Iran's economy. But Mossadegh and the hardliners would accept nothing less than full Iranian ownership of its oil facilities.

Relations between Iran and the West further deteriorated in 1952 because of Mossadegh's socialist reforms and concern over his deepening relationship with Iran's communist, Soviet-influenced **Tudeh Party**. Mossadegh's opponents within Iran were also deeply troubled over the prime minister's increasingly despotic rule.[133]

A year later, the British under Prime Minister Winston Churchill and the Americans under President Dwight D. Eisenhower collaborated on a plot (code-named **Operation Ajax**) to overthrow the regime and restore the Shah to power. Western covert action blended with local discontent on the streets of Tehran on August 19, 1953 in the form of a massive pro-monarchy/anti-Mossadegh protest. The pro-Shah faction stormed the capital and bombarded Mossadegh's home until the prime minister surrendered and was arrested. The Shah, who had been living in temporary exile in Rome, returned to Iran, deposed Mossadegh and reclaimed his authority as Iran's leader.

Flow of Oil Resumes
Upon returning to power, the Shah reversed Mossadegh's policies and agreed to divide ownership of the **Anglo-Persian Oil Company** (which later became **British Petroleum**) among eight companies: 40% of the shares would be divided equally among 5 major American companies, British Petroleum retained a 40% share, Royal Dutch Shell received 14% and the last 6% would go to the French

---

[131] Egyptian leader Gamal Abdel Nasser nationalized the Suez Canal in 1956.

[132] Only Japan and Italy ignored Britain's threats by continuing to buy Iranian oil.

[133] The Shah had forced Mossadegh to resign as prime minister in 1952 but the decision was met with public outrage and the Shah was obliged to reinstate him. Mossadegh took advantage of his popularity by getting the Shah to give him full control of the military and convincing the Majles to increase his political powers.

CFP with Iran receiving a share of the profits. Within a few years, the Consortium helped bring Iran's oil production back to its pre-nationalization level.

In 1970, the Consortium Agreement was revised, giving Iran 55% of the profits and, three years later, the Shah announced that Iran would take over the Consortium altogether thereby completing Mossadegh's nationalization begun 22 years earlier.

By that time, international demand for petroleum had outgrown the supply, giving the oil-producing countries considerable leverage in international trade.

1970s
On October 6, 1973, the date of Yom Kippur, the holiest Jewish holiday, Egypt and Syria launched a surprise attack on Israel setting off the **Yom Kippur/Ramadan/October War**. The next day the Arab states imposed an embargo on oil sales to the United States because of America's support of Israel. Iran, which, at the time, was on good terms with Israel and the United States, did not join the embargo but used the opportunity to increase its own production and significantly raise oil prices (from $1.80 a barrel in 1970 to $2.90 in mid 1973 to $11.65 after the October Yom Kippur War).

As a result, Iran was suddenly awash with money while Americans were waiting in gas lines to buy gasoline at much inflated prices.

To balance things out, the Shah spent billions of dollars buying top-of-the-line American weaponry, tanks, radars and other military equipment to supply Iran's newly expanded armed forces. The Shah also bought eight large nuclear power plants to ease Iran's growing power needs since the country's existing power grids could not handle the surge in the demand for electricity.

The new oil money helped fund a number of government projects and a corps of bureaucratic government workers, but it also led to inflation, corruption and a widening gap between the class of very wealthy Iranians and the rest of the population who couldn't afford to buy the luxurious consumer goods that had flooded the market.

Popular discontent had come to a fever pitch in 1979 when the **Ayatollah Khomeini** returned to Iran vowing to rid the country of foreigners and force their puppet, the Shah, to abdicate.

1979 Revolution
The last of Iran's foreign oil workers[134] left "**The Fields**" (the main production area) of **Masjid-i-Sulemian** at the end of 1978 in the midst of chaos, and Iranian oil exports came to a complete stop on December 25, 1978.

The loss of Iran's oil in the world market caused an international panic resulting, again, in price controls, rationing, long lines at the gas pumps in the U.S. and a scramble to find new sources of oil (including exploring the production

---

[134] The Oil Service Company of Iran (OSCO), which had taken over from the consortium after the Shah's return, was mostly staffed by foreign oil men from the member companies.

of "synthetic fuels" made from coal). Saudi Arabia and other OPEC countries increased their oil production to compensate for the decline before
Iranian oil exports resumed at the beginning of March 1979, but the upheaval
had already caused spikes in gas prices and stirred political tensions.

Hostage Crisis

After his downfall, the exiled Shah searched for a country that would take
him. U.S. President **Jimmy Carter** initially refused to let Iran's former
leader settle in the United States for fear of aggravating the new Islamic
regime but had a change of heart when news about the severity of the Shah's
cancer and need for medical treatment reached the White House.

The Shah was admitted into the United States to undergo treatment temporarily and on the condition that he leave as soon as he was medically able.

In Iran, however, the move was seen as another ploy by the United States to orches-
trate a regime change like it had in 1953 (when the CIA had helped depose
Mossadegh and reinstall the Shah). In retaliation, a group of students occupied the
American Embassy – by that time managed by a skeleton staff of only 63
Americans. On November 12, 1979, fifty two American embassy workers were
taken hostage by the Iranian students, prompting President Carter to freeze Iranian
assets and impose an embargo on the import of Iranian oil to the United States.

The oil embargo didn't harm Iran, which simply sold the commodity to other
buyers, but it did result in the redistribution of supplies around the world.

Iran-Iraq War 1980

On September 22, 1980, Iraq invaded Iran. The war was declared for a number of reasons: Iraq's fear that the Shi'ite Islamic revolution in Iran would
spread among Iraq's own Shi'ite majority; the struggle for dominance of the
Islamic world; rivalry between Iraqi President Saddam Hussein and the
Ayatollah Khomeini (who had been expelled from Iran just a few years earlier); Iran's support for the Kurds and, of course, oil.

Iraq's official declaration of war against Iran centered on control of the **Shatt-
al-Arab** waterway – the main shipping route that connects the Iraqi city of
Basra to the Persian Gulf and through which most of Iraq's oil is transported.

The Iraqis also hoped to capture the Iranian province of **Khuzestan** (home to
the main oil-producing cities of **Abadan** and **Masjid-i-Suleiman**) and to incite
the mainly Arab-speaking occupants[135] to rebel against the Iranian government
(it didn't work). For Saddam Hussein, the goal was to appropriate Iran's oil.

The Iranian city of **Abadan** was overrun by Iraqis in the first days of the war.
Although the city was never captured, the sustained siege and subsequent bombing
caused terrible damage to the oil refinery. Production at the oil refinery didn't resume

---

[135] Arabs first invaded Khuzestan from Basra in A.D. 639. In the 16th century, an Arab tribe
from Kuwait, the Bani Kaab, settled in the area followed by subsequent waves of Arab
immigrants in later years.

for another 13 years and only reached its pre-war level of production in 1997. The Iranians counterattacked against Iraqi facilities reducing Iraqi oil exports to only 1.8 million barrels per day (BPD) from 3.2 million barrels before the war. Altogether, the war removed almost 4 million daily barrels of oil from the world market.

In the mid-1980s, the Iran-Iraq conflict moved to the Persian Gulf – one of the most strategic waterways in the world due to its importance in world oil transportation – initiating a phase of the conflict known as the '**tanker war**." Beginning in 1984, Iran and Iraq began attacking neutral oil tankers (Kuwaiti tankers in particular) carrying oil from the rival countries hoping to force them to stop aiding the enemy. By 1986, more than 100 ships had been sunk or damaged compelling the Western nations to send naval ships to the region in order to keep the tankers moving and safe from attack.

In 1988, as abruptly as the war had started, Iran and Iraq declared a cease-fire.

Gulf War
Both Iran and Iraq eagerly wanted to rebuild their countries after 8 years of war but both had sustained great damage to their oil producing facilities — their primary source of export revenue. The situation was aggravated in 1986 when the price of oil plunged.[136]

Iraq hoped to raise oil prices to help pay back their war debt (including $14 billion owed to Kuwait) by convincing the OPEC countries to reduce production. Instead, Kuwait, Iraq's neighbor raised production causing prices to fall even lower. Iraq also accused Kuwait of stealing its oil by "slant-drilling" to extract oil from Iraqi oil wells.

In order to help stimulate Iraq's economy, draw tension away from internal problems, seize Kuwaiti oil, force countries to forgive Iraqi debts and settle an age-old border dispute, Saddam Hussein decided to invade Kuwait, setting off the Gulf War. The Iraqis were forced to withdraw from Kuwait in early 1991 by a coalition of forces led by the United Nations. As the Iraqi troops left Kuwait, though, they made a last-ditch effort to reduce oil output by setting fire to 500 Kuwaiti oil wells. The fires took more than a year to quell and caused a great deal of environmental damage.

Iran today
By 1993, Abadan's oil refinery had been rebuilt and production levels reached pre-war levels a few years later. Today, Iran produces more than three million barrels of oil a day, which is still a far cry from the 6-8 million barrels a day it produced in 1974.

The lower output is due both to damage caused during the Iran-Iraq War and the fact that it acts in compliance with its quota set by OPEC.
In order to increase or even maintain its output capacity, Iran needs to invest billions of dollars to repair the damaged oil fields and petrochemical facili-

---

[136] Price decreases were the result of increased oil production in Saudi Arabia in mid-1985.

ties and modernize functioning facilities. Since Iran was one of the first countries to extract oil, most of the oil near the surface has already been drilled and what is left requires sophisticated machinery to extract.[137]

Iran's oil industry has also suffered from mismanagement and corruption since foreign managers left Iran in 1979. Article 81 of Iran's 1980 constitution expressly forbids the "granting of concessions to foreigners" or the "formation of companies or institutions dealing with commerce, industry, agriculture, service, or mineral extraction" which restricts the participation of foreign companies in Iran's reconstruction.

Externally, American sanctions have also taken their toll by threatening penalties against any nation that invests more than $20 million per year in Iran's oil industry (see ILSA in Sanctions section). The aim was to target Iran's greatest source of foreign currency thereby hindering Iran's ability to fund terrorist activity or develop weapons of mass destruction.

Nuclear Energy
Iran's internal consumption of oil and gas is growing faster than Iran can accommodate forcing the country to import refined oil products. Since oil exports account for more than 80% of Iran's income earned by exports and provides a steady stream of hard currency (which Iran needs to buy international products), the government is trying to lessen Iranian consumption of the valuable commodity by employing nuclear power for Iran's energy needs.

Iran is also trying to develop other export products (handmade carpets and dried fruits are Iran's second and third largest exports after oil[138]) to lessen reliance on oil for export income.

Importance of Iranian oil
Most of America's supply of crude oil comes from U.S. production (35%) and the rest is imported from Canada, Mexico, Saudi Arabia, Venezuela and other countries. But even though the U.S. isn't directly dependent on Iran for its oil supply, any drastic changes in that country's supply or production could greatly affect the United States and the rest of the world.

Japan, which has no oil of its own, relies on Iran for 17% of its oil imports.[139] Iran also supplied about 13% of China's oil in 2003 and the demand for oil in China has continued to rise. Any disruption to the flow of Iran's oil could thus destabilize countries that provide the United States with almost a quarter of its total imports (China, 14%, Japan 9%).

A decrease in Iran's oil production (Iran is the fourth largest oil producer in

---

[137] The traditional "natural-lift method" no longer works as well since the pressure in underground reservoirs is diminishing. Iran now needs to pump gas or water back into the reservoir to keep the overall pressure up. But that process could eventually damage the reservoirs.

[138] In 1994, oil and gas amounted to 82.3% of Iran's export products, carpets were 6.6% and fresh and dried fruits (especially pistachio nuts) equaled 3.3%

[139] Thirty percent of Japan's oil comes from Saudi Arabia and 29% comes from the United Arab Emirates.

the world) could also affect worldwide prices by affecting the balance of supply-and-demand.[140]

Furthermore, because Iran is strategically situated along the northern border of the Persian Gulf, it could easily obstruct passage through the **Strait of Hormuz**, the narrow waterway through which 40% of the world's oil exports pass daily from the oil fields of Saudi Arabia, Kuwait, Iraq and the United Arab Emirates.

Petrodollars vs. Petroeuros

Since World War II, the price of oil has been denominated in U.S. dollars ("petrodollars") giving the United States a great advantage; first because fluctuations in the value of the dollar have had no direct effect on the price of oil for Americans; secondly because oil-importing countries need to have a supply of dollars in order to purchase oil[141] ensuring that the dollar remains the strongest currency in the world.

If the situation changed and oil was suddenly priced in euros instead of dollars, the effect on the United States would be devastating. Countries would immediately try to dump their supply of U.S. dollars causing the value of the dollar to plummet and the price of foreign imports to America to go up. A devalued dollar would significantly increase America's foreign debt and the United States would have much less influence on OPEC and other international institutions.

When Saddam Hussein declared that Iraq was no longer going to accept U.S. dollars for Iraq's oil in 2000, the threat that other OPEC countries would follow suit became a considerable concern to the United States – undoubtedly influencing the government's decision to go to war with Iraq in 2003. Just months after U.S. troops secured control over Iraq, the price for Iraqi oil on the international market was converted back from the euro to the dollar.

In 2005, Iran decided that it was going to begin accepting only euros for its oil in 2006and create an **Iranian Oil Bourse** (IOB) (an oil stock exchange) that could compete with the London and New York dollar-denominated oil exchanges. The move would greatly benefit Iran's biggest trading partners in the European Union and deal a major blow to Iran's rival, America. The IOB could make Iran a major hub for oil deals in the region undercutting the two leadin oil exchanges, New York's NYMEX and London't International Petroleum Exchange (IPE).

---

[140] Less availability to oil would make the commodity more valuable causing the price per barrel of oil to increase.

[141] Currently about 70% of all currency reserves are in American dollars and approximately $3 trillion in worldwide circulation is directly tied to petrodollars.

IRAN AND TERRORISM

Spreading the Revolution and supporting "Freedom Fighters"

When the clerical revolutionaries overthrew the Shah and his alleged puppeteer, America (the "Great Satan"), to build an Islamic Republic, they believed that were doing "God's work on earth" by building "an ideal Islamic society that could be a model for all people of the world."[142] With that in mind, the authors of the nation's constitution incorporated the aim of "fulfilling the ideological mission of *jihad* [Islamic holy war]" by "extending the sovereignty of God's law throughout the world."

In Articles 3 and 154 of the constitution, the revolutionaries further proclaimed the "unsparing support to the freedom fighters of the world ... against the oppressors in every corner of the globe" as one of Iran's primary state goals.

The ambition to spread the revolution and to aid "freedom fighters" in their struggles against oppressors has shaped Iran's foreign policy since the early 1980s and conveniently served the nation's political aims. Their support for militant Muslims around the world, however, has also earned Iran the internationally dishonorable position of being one of the world's most active state sponsors of terrorism costing the country lucrative trade and keeping Iran isolated.

LEBANESE HEZBOLLAH

Since the 1980s Iran's most visible association with terrorism has been through its support of the Shi'a fundamentalist group, Lebanon's **Hezbollah**.

In order to accommodate Lebanon's diverse population, political power was divided among various ethnic and religious communities. The amount of representation each group received was based on a census taken in the 1930s. After 50 years of demographic shifts, though, certain groups had grown while others had shrunk in number. Lebanon's Shi'a population, which had become the largest bloc in the country by the 1980s, for example, had found itself under-represented in the contemporary government.

Initially, many Shi'as joined **AMAL** (Afwaj al-Muqawamah al-Lubnaniyya or "Battalions of the Lebanese Resistance")[143] a moderate secular organization formed to advance Shi'a interests in Lebanon. In time, though, religious Lebanese Shi'ites looking for more radical representation broke away from AMAL to form their own organizations. In the late 1970s, they were joined by a number of Lebanese Islamic extremists who had been kicked out of Iraq where they had been studying in prominent Shi'a seminaries.[144]

Iran's Islamic Revolution in 1979 greatly inspired the Shi'as in Lebanon who

---

[142] Quoted from a translation of Iran's constitution.

[143] "Amal" also means "hope" in Arabic.

[144] To secure their power, the newly installed Baathist party of Iraq expelled all foreign-born Muslim extremists seen as a political threat.

quickly joined Iran's Revolutionary Guards Corps in that country.

For the Iranians, having a friendly outpost in Lebanon allowed the Persians to maintain a foothold in the Levant,[145] in the same way friendly relations with Israel served United States interests in the area. In order to serve their western outpost, the Iranians supported their Shi'ite Lebanese allies by providing training, money, weapons, an intelligence network and social services. In 1982, Iran's Revolutionary Guard (IRGC) created a Lebanese "**Hezbollah**"[146] to coordinate activities and distribute resources.

Lebanese Hezbollah, which conducted a vast number of attacks against Israelis, shared Iran's commitment to drive Israelis out of what Hezbollah and Iran considered to be Palestinian territory. (See Box pg. 74)

ISRAEL

In **Ayatollah Ruhollah Khomeini's** estimation, America, the "Great Satan," had a little brother, the "Little Satan," or **Israel** – and Khomeini's arch nemesis, the Shah, had been friendly with both of them.

In the face of common threats — the Soviet Union and Arab radicals — the Shah of Iran and Israel had decided to strengthen ties with the United States and with each other. In the 1950s, Israel was still struggling for survival as a new nation (created in 1948) in a very hostile neighborhood. In 1952, Arab nationalist **Gamal Abdel Nasser** had overthrown Egypt's king and allied himself with the Soviet Union. A few years later, Syria joined with Egypt to form the **United Arab Republic (UAR)** and the two worked to incorporate other Arab nations into the alliance. Contesting Nasser's collective influence over the Arab countries was the new **Baathist** regime in Iraq (soon to be headed by **Saddam Hussein**).

The banding together of the Arab nations (Iran was ethnically "Persian"), and their Soviet ties as well as the overthrow of both Egypt's king and Iraq's Hashemite monarchical dynasty threatened Iran's own hereditary monarch, the Shah, who looked to the U.S. and its ally, Israel, for support.

Thirty years later, the Shah's relationship with the State of Israel[147] was held as one of the most urgent reasons for his overthrow. The Zionists'[148] seizure of Palestinian lands in the Levant, according to Khomeini, was just the first step in a grander plan to take over all Middle East territory, spread corruption and ultimately destroy Islam. It was, therefore, the duty of all Muslim states to support the Palestinian "freedom fighters" to prevent Israel from accomplishing this goal.

---

[145] The nations along the eastern shore of the Mediterranean Sea including Cyprus, Egypt, Israel, Lebanon, Syria and Turkey make up the Levant.

[146] In Iran, pro-Islamic Republic forces called themselves "Hezbollah" without any political affiliation.

[147] Israel maintained a virtual embassy in Tehran. When the CIA dropped its support of SAVAK, Israel's secret service, **Mossad**, was employed to help train Iran's loathed secret service agency.

[148] Khomeini was careful to distinguish "Zionists" from "Jews" who, he claimed, are "a nation like any other nation." "Zionists" are Jews who support the establishment of a Jewish homeland in Palestine. The term was coined in 1891 to describe the 19th political movement begun by Theodore Herzl. "Zion" is the name of a hill in Jerusalem and means "marker" in Hebrew.

Along with the fulfillment of Iran's own constitutionally-mandated state aims – that is, to spread the revolution and support Islamic "freedom fighters" worldwide — Iran's presence in the Middle East and its call for nations to unite against the "Zionist Imperialists" also played into Iran's ambition to head the international community of Muslims. By creating a pan-Islamic movement (which would include both Arab and Persian Muslims) Iran could compete with exclusive pan-Arab movements.

By supporting **Hezbollah**, and later, **Islamic Jihad** (largely a cover-name for Hezbollah operatives) and **HAMAS** (the religious alternative to the **Palestinian Liberation Organization** [PLO] headed by **Yasser Arafat** until his death in November 2004), and other anti-Israeli militants, Iran was able to fight the "Little Satan" (Israel) without committing its own troops.

Lebanon's 1982 War and Hostages
In 1982, Israel invaded Lebanon in order to get rid of the PLO (which had been launching attacks on Israel from its Lebanese bases since the 1970s),[149] to avenge the assassination of **Shlomo Argov**, Israel's ambassador to London, and to help set up a government in Lebanon dominated by their allies, the Christian **Maronites**. A **multi-national force** (MNF) of Americans, British, French and Italian troops was deployed to supervise the peaceful departure of PLO troops and to prevent outbreaks of violence among Lebanon's civilian population.

What Iran saw, however, was Israel's encroachment into Muslim territory in order to install a Christian government with the backing of Israel's co-religionist Christian allies (U.S., U.K., France, Italy). In response, Iran sent 1,000 Revolutionary Guards to arm Lebanese Shi'as to drive the Israelis and the Western foreigners out of the country.

What followed was a decade of terrorist attacks against Westerners which included the world's first truck bomb detonated outside the U.S. Embassy in April 1983, leaving 61 people dead, another suicide truck bombing in the middle of the U.S. Marines complex in Beirut in October 1983, killing 39 people, and the hijacking of a TWA airline on its way from Athens to New York.

In 1985 **Reverend Lawrence Martin Jenco**, the director of Catholic Relief Services, was the first in a string of Westerners who were kidnapped in Beirut by militants claiming to be members of **Islamic Jihad** (an oft-used cover-name for radical Islamists inspired by the Iran's Islamic Republic).[150]

---

[149] The PLO had been based in Lebanon since their expulsion from Jordan in 1975. For more on Israel, Palestine and Lebanon see Roraback's Israel-Palestine in a Nutshell.

[150] The name "Islamic Jihad" was used by a number of organizations inspired by Iran's 1979 Revolution and the rise of Islamic militancy in the Middle East in the 1970s and 80s. Today, though, the name is primarily associated with the Palestinian Islamic Jihad (PIJ) created by Fathi Shaqaqi in the early 1980s.

Iran-Contra Affair

After more high-profile Americans were kidnapped (among them, **Terry Anderson**, the chief Middle East correspondent for the Associated Press, David Jacobsen, director of the American University Hospital in Beirut and American educator Thomas Sutherland), the Lebanese hostage crisis had turned into a political quagmire for U.S. President **Ronald Reagan**. Like former President **Jimmy Carter** during the 1979 American Embassy hostage crisis, President Reagan was eager to get the hostages released without appearing to submit to the terrorists.

He had his opportunity in 1985 when Israeli officials suggested that a transfer of American arms to Iran could lead to the release of American hostages held in Lebanon. Although Israel and Iran were enemies, the Israelis recognized that Iraq posed a greater threat. The Israelis hoped the weapons would help tilt the odds in Iran's favor in the course of the 1980-88 Iran-Iraq war. However, Israel was not permitted to send U.S.-made weapons to another country without American consent.

A month later, the first planeload of American-made weapons was secretly sent from Israel to Iran. Profits from the sales were then sent to aid the U.S.-backed **Contras** who were fighting to overthrow the **Sandinista** regime in Nicaragua.

Despite the terms of the **arms-for-hostages** swap, few Americans were, in fact, set free. Even when Americans were released, more hostages were taken, keeping the numbers stable. The deal with the terrorists had been a failure.

The whole surreptitious transaction was exposed in an article in a Lebanese magazine and picked up by news agencies worldwide, turning the newly dubbed "**Iran-Contra Affair**" into a political public relations nightmare for the Reagan administration.

The last of the Western hostages were not freed until mid-1992.

Iran and the Middle East Peace Treaty

Worldwide events in the 1990s greatly affected Iran's international relations. By 1991, the Soviet Union had disintegrated into a number of smaller states, Saddam Hussein had invaded Kuwait sparking the Gulf War and U.S. President **Bill Clinton** was helping Israel and its neighbors construct a lasting peace treaty.

The collapse of the Soviet Union followed by the independence of former Islamic republics (Turkmenistan, Uzbekistan, Kazakhstan, and Azerbaijan) just north of Iran eliminated the threat of war with the U.S.S.R.. During the upheaval, caches of Soviet-style weapons suddenly came on the market at greatly reduced prices.

Saddam Hussein, meanwhile, invaded Kuwait in order to force the country to forgive Iraq's war-debts, to redirect the attention of Iraq's population in the wake of the costly Iran-Iraq war and to curb Kuwait's oil production capacity in order to lift oil prices among other reasons.

The speed, strength and ease of America's response to the invasion – the

United States and its 38-nation coalition (including many Muslim countries) crushed Saddam's forces in six weeks and showed what the U.S. could accomplish when it was determined causing Iran to fear the consequences if the Islamic Republic became the next target.

The Gulf War had affected Israel (which had endured Scud Missile attacks deployed from Iraq during the conflict) and highlighted the need for a resolution to the Middle East crisis, believed to lie at the core of all conflicts in the region. Israel's feelings of vulnerability and then-U.S. President **George H. Bush's** determination to resolve the Israeli-Palestinian conflict prompted the first in a series of peace talks between Israel's Prime Minister **Yitzhak Shamir** and delegates from Syria, Lebanon, Jordan and Egypt in Madrid, Spain in October 1991.

Clinton took up the peace process when he came to office in 1993 by arranging the **Oslo Accords** that had ended dramatically with a historic handshake in Washington D.C. between PLO leader **Yasser Arafat** and Israeli Prime Minister **Yitzhak Rabin** (who had succeeded **Shamir** in 1992).

But the prospect of peace between Israel and Iran's Arab allies was a great threat to the Islamic Republic. For one thing, the Iranians still considered Israel an imperial nation illegally constructed by the Christian West on Islamic lands. The peace process, in contrast, aimed to legitimize Israel's existence.

Moreover, if Syria (one of Iran's closest allies) made peace with Israel, the leaders would likely curb Hezbollah activities hindering Iran's influence in Lebanon and the region.

Iranian Foreign Policy 1990s

In the face of the new threats following the Gulf War and with the peace process going forward at full speed, Iran decided to cultivate its relationship with like-minded states and organizations to counter America and its allies (Egypt, Jordan, Turkey, Israel and others). In this pursuit, Iran stepped up its support for co-religionist "freedom fighters" around the world.

Iran was suspected of aiding the **Egyptian Islamic Jihad** and Egypt's largest militant group, **Gama'at al-Islamiyya** which aimed to overthrow the Egyptian government and replace it with an Islamic state.[151] Algeria's government accused Iran of supporting **Algerian extremists**. Iran purportedly gave aid to the **Kurdistan Workers' Party (PKK)** — a Marxist-Leninist insurgent group of Turkish Kurds seeking to establish an independent Kurdish state in southeastern Turkey.[152] And Iran provided military aid to **Sudan's Islamic regime** in the early 1990s while the country was

---

[151] Al-Gama'at has attacked Egyptian government officials and opponents of Islamic extremism and has launched attacks on tourists in Egypt since 1992.

[152] PKK has attacked Turkish diplomatic and commercial facilities in cities in Western Europe and tried to damage Turkey's tourist industry by bombing tourist sites and hotels and kidnapping foreigners.

engaged in a brutal civil war between the mainly Muslim north and the Animist and Christian south. [153] Iran also helped the **Islamic Movement of Uzbekistan** (IMU) (which wanted to overthrow Uzbekistani President **Karimov** and establish an Islamic state in Uzbekistan) as well as **Bahrain's** Shi'ite oppositionists against the country's Sunni **al-Khalifa** ruling family.

Most damaging to the Middle East Peace process was Iran's increased support for **Hezbollah, Palestinian Islamic Jihad (PIJ)** and **HAMAS.** Empowered by Iran's aid and encouragement, the organizations accelerated terrorist attacks on Israel while the Jewish nation was trying to negotiate the terms of the Middle East Peace treaty. As planned, the violence also affected Israel's voters who soon lost faith in Israeli Prime Minister **Shimon Peres's** diplomatic approach to the Middle East Peace treaty. The series of attacks staged by the pro-Palestinian groups just before the elections consequently compelled voters to vote against **Peres** and in favor of the more aggressive militant candidate, **Benjamin Netanyahu**. Predictably, soon after Netanyahu came to office, the peace talks came to a halt.

Israelis feared an alliance between Hamas, which came to power after the January 2006 Palestinian elections and Iran after Hamas' exiled senior political leader, Khaled Meshaal met with Iranian President Mahmoud Ahmadinejad soon after Hamas' victory. Some analysts, though, claimed that a close relationship was unlikely because of distrust of Iran's Shi'ite leaders by Hamas' Sunni leaders and because of Hamas' nationalist nature.

TERRORIST ORGANIZATIONS

Palestinian Islamic Jihad:
An alliance of loosely affiliated militant Palestinian factions formed in the 1970s and committed to the creation of an Islamic Palestinian state and the destruction of Israel. They also oppose moderate Arab governments which they believe have been tainted by Western secularism.

Hezbollah: (also known as **Islamic Jihad,** the **Organization of the Oppressed on Earth, Ansar Allah** and other names). An anti-American, anti-Israeli Shi'a Muslim group formed in Lebanon and dedicated to the creation of an Iranian-style Islamic republic in Lebanon.

HAMAS (**Harakat al-Muqawama al-Islamiya** or "**Islamic Resistance Movement**"): Formed in the late 1980s as an outgrowth of the Palestinian branch of the **Muslim Brotherhood,** HAMAS has been dedicated to the establishment of an Islamic Palestinian state in place of Israel. The group served as an Islamic alternative to Yasser Arafat's secular **Palestinian Liberation Organization** (PLO) which had in 1993 abandoned its cause for the destruction of Israel favoring instead a "two-state" solution (that is, the creation of two co-existing states - Israeli and Palestinian Authority). HAMAS has also provided welfare and social services for poor Palestinians, funded by donations from Muslims around the world.

---

[153] The goal of the Iran-Sudan alliance was to spread radical Islam fundamentalism. In 1991, Sudan's leader, **General al-Bashir**, enacted the **Criminal Act** of 1991 that instituted harsh Islamic punishments and provided a possible future application of Islamic Law *(Sharia)* in the non-Muslim south. **Osama bin Laden** (the mastermind behind the September 11, 2001 terrorist attack on the U.S.) lived in Sudan from 1991 until he was expelled in 1996.

Khobar Towers

On June 25, 1996, a truck bomb was detonated at the site of the **Khobar Towers** housing complex in Saudi Arabia, a facility that housed American military personnel stationed there to defend Saudi Arabia against Iraqi assault after the Gulf War, killing 19 Americans and wounding 372.

The Americans strongly believed that the bombers were members of a group called the **Hezbollah al-Hijaz (the Party of God of the Hijaz)**[154] created, trained and supported by the **Iranian Revolutionary Guard (IRGC)**. But the U.S. didn't have enough evidence to make their case in a court of law and the Saudis, who did have overwhelming evidence that Iran was involved, were not forthcoming[155] (the incriminating evidence wasn't released until 1999).

ILSA (See Sanctions section)

Without evidence, the only recourse the United States had against Iran, which had attacked the Middle East peace process and continued to support terrorists around the world, was to penalize the country economically.

About a month after the Khobar Tower incident, the U.S. Congress voted to punish all non-U.S. companies that invested more than $20 million in Iran's oil industry. The bill (called the **Iran-Libya Sanctions Act** of 1996 or **ILSA**) was put into effect on July 23, 1996 despite the intense disapproval of the European Union.

Khatami

Iran's foreign policy changed slightly when **President Khatami** came to power in 1997. Although Iran's new president echoed his predecessors' opposition to the Middle East peace process and general animosity to the West, he favored a more conciliatory approach to the situation. In CNN interviews, Khatami declared that Iran would not "impose [its] views on others or stand in their way" when referring to the peace agreement and when tourists were targeted by Egyptian organizations he condemned all attacks on innocent civilians.

Khatami's power in Iran's government, though, was soon overshadowed by the country's religious leaders and Iran continued to support Hezbollah and other militant groups.

Iran and Al Qaeda

Iran's relationship with Afghanistan fluctuated throughout the 20th century depending on the regime that was in power.

Iran opposed the Soviet government that ruled Afghanistan in 1979 and helped support the ten-year Afghan *mujaheddin* resistance movement.

---

[154] Muslims who reject the Saudi family's sovereignty over Arabia refer to the western part of the country by its traditional name, the **Hijaz**.

[155] The Saudis were afraid that the United States would launch a military strike against Iran in retaliation which would damage Saudi Arabia's relationship with Iran and give the Americans more reason to station troops in the Middle East. The Saudis also feared that, as in Iraq during the Gulf War, the Americans would leave Iran's regime (like Saddam Hussein's) intact and able to counterattack.

Iran also rejected the **Taliban**, a fundamentalist group of Islamic students who took power a few months after the Soviets were expelled in 1989, because of their harsh treatment of Afghanistan's Shi'a minority. Iran's diplomatic relations with the Taliban especially deteriorated after 1998 when Taliban forces seized the Iranian consulate in the Afghan city of **Mazar-e-Sharif** and executed Iranian diplomats. Until the fall of the Taliban in 2001, the Iranians supported the Taliban's rivals, the **Northern Alliance**.[156]

As for **al-Qaeda**, the Islamic militant umbrella organization developed by **Osama bin Laden** in Afghanistan during the war with the Soviets, the Iranians shared the group's hatred of common foes, the United States, Israel and Saudi Arabia, but diverged over the organization's aggressive tactics and religious ideology (Al-Qaeda members are primarily Sunni while Iran is a Shi'a Muslim nation).

The Iranians officially denounced al-Qaeda-organized terrorist strikes on New York City's World Trade Center, the Pentagon and other potential targets on September 11, 2001. Candlelight vigils were even held throughout Iran in sympathy for the American victims of the attack.

The **9/11 Commission Report** published in 2004, however, claimed that many of the hijackers responsible for the September 11 assaults had passed through Iran before the attacks and that Iran had a history of allowing al-Qaeda members to enter and exit Iran across the Afghan border. The report also suggested that Iranian officials had approached al-Qaeda leadership in 1994 to propose a collaborative relationship in future attacks on the United States but were turned down by Osama bin Laden. There was even suspicion that al-Qaeda might have collaborated with **Hezbollah** and its Iranian sponsors in the 1996 bombing of the Khobar Towers – although no firm conclusions were made.

Axis of Evil
In his State of the Union address in January 2002, U.S. President **George W. Bush** announced that Iran, along with Iraq and North Korea, constituted an "Axis of Evil."

North Korea was included because, according to President Bush, "its regime was arming with missiles and weapons of mass destruction, while starving its citizens;" Iraq, because the country "continued to flaunt its hostility toward America and to support terror;" and Iran because it "aggressively pursued [weapons of mass destruction] and export terror, while an unelected few repressed the Iranian people's hope for freedom."

Indeed, the United States has been particularly uneasy about Iran's apparent progress towards building nuclear weapons (see section on Iran's Nuclear Program, pg. 50), its ongoing support for Hezbollah and other violent organizations, its avowed hatred of the United States and its dedication to the destruction of Israel.

---

[156] For more of Afghanistan, see Roraback's <u>Afghanistan in a Nutshell</u>

HEZBOLLAH (Brief)

Name: "Party of God"
Founded: 1982
Origin: Formed from a number of radical Shi'a groups in Lebanon shortly after Israel's invasion of Lebanon in 1982.
Relationship with Iran: Hezbollah was conceived by Iran and aided initially by Iran's Revolutionary Guards. Although Iran denies involvement in Hezbollah-sponsored terrorist activity, Iran has been a close ally, financial backer and arms supplier. Iran considers Hezbollah a resistance organization dedicated to liberating Lebanon from Israeli occupation and helping liberate the Palestinians from Israeli occupation. Syria is also a sponsor.
Other alliances: Syria has supplied Hezbollah with weapons
Purpose: To fight Israel in southern Lebanon, to create a Muslim fundamentalist state modeled on Iran, and rid Lebanon of Israeli and Western forces. Hezbollah supports the destruction of the state of Israel and cooperates with other militant Islamic organizations that share their goal.
Composition: Hezbollah was created to serve Lebanon's religious Shi'a community. It is estimated to have a core membership of several 1000 militants and activists.
Leadership: *Spiritual leader.* **Sheikh Mohammed Hussein Fadlallah.** *Key planner*: **Imad Fayez Mugniyah**
Military Wing: Al-Muqawwama al-Islamiyya ("Islamic Resistance")
Civilian arm: Hezbollah provides a number of social services for 1,000s of Lebanese Shi'ites. The organization runs hospitals, schools, agricultural services and orphanages and owns a newspaper, TV and radio station.
Political role: Since the May 2005 elections Hezbollah has held 23 seats in Lebanon's 128-member parliament.
Terrorism:
Hezbollah has been designated a terrorist organization by the United States, the United Kingdom, Canada, Australia and other Western countries.
Hezbollah is believed to have caused the deaths of more than 800 people and been behind nearly 200 attacks including:
* Series of kidnappings of many Western hostages in Lebanon in the 1980s.
* Suicide truck bombing of U.S. embassy in Beirut in 1983 (63 people killed)
* Attack on the U.S. Marine barracks in Beirut in 1983 (200 U.S. Marines killed)
* 1985 hijacking of TWA Flight 847
* Two major attacks on Jewish targets in Argentina
        -- 1992 bombing of the Israeli Embassy (29 killed)
        -- 1994 bombing of Jewish community center (95 killed)
* 1994 Panamanian flight bombing (12 killed)
Hezbollah has denied involvement in these attacks.
Affiliations
Purportedly shares members with Palestinian Islamic Jihad and is an ally of Hamas. Possible contacts with Al Qaeda.[a]

[a] Al-Qaeda and the Taliban consider Shi'ites heretics and have attacked Shi'as in Afghanistan and elsewhere. Hezbollah's leader, Fadlallah, in turn, condemned the Sept. 11, 2001 attacks in New York City and Washington D.C.

IRAN-IRAQ RELATIONS

Arabs and Persians have been military rivals since ancient times and religious opponents since the split between Islamic **Shi'ite** and **Sunnis** in the 7th century. (See Islam section, pg. 39)

After the fall of the **Ottoman Empire** at the conclusion of World War I, the British created the new country of **Iraq** by joining the three Ottoman *vilayets* (provinces) of **Basra**, which was primarily Shi'ite, **Baghdad**, inhabited by Sunnis, and Kurdish **Mosul**. To rule over the predominantly Shi'ite country[157] the British installed a **Sunni** king from Arabia – in large part to assuage Britain's Sunni-Muslim Arab allies and to ensure that the monarch remained weak and dependent on the British. **Sunni** political dominance in Iraq was maintained with the rise of **Saddam Hussein** and challenged after he was deposed by the Americans in 2003.

For the first time in decades, Shi'ites from Iran could freely visit Shi'ism's holiest cities of **Kerbala**, Iraq where **Prophet Muhammad's** grandson, **Husayn,** was killed in A.D. 680 and **Najaf** where the Prophet's son-in-law, **Ali**, was buried. Saddam Hussein, who lived in constant fear that Iraq's Shi'as would one day stage a popular rebellion against his regime, blocked access to the holy cities forcing Iran's Shi'ite scholars to develop their spiritual center in the city of **Qom**, Iran.

Despite the restrictions, though, tens of thousands of Shi'as tried to make pilgrimages to the holy Shi'ite shrines in **Kerbala** and **Najaf** every year. Among them was the **Grand Ayatollah Khomeini** who had been exiled from Iran by **Muhammad Reza Shah** in 1964 and who resided in **Najaf** until he was expelled by **Saddam Hussein** in 1978. The deportation resulted in a bitter enmity between Hussein and Khomeini from that point on.

Iran-Iraq War
When Khomeini came to power in Iran after the Islamic Revolution in 1979, Iran and Iraq engaged in a number of skirmishes over control of the disputed **Shatt al-Arab** waterway which connects the Tigris and Euphrates Rivers to the Persian Gulf. The dispute became the pretext for open warfare in September 1980.

One of the main triggers for the Iran-Iraq war was Saddam's fear that Iraq's religious Shi'ites would be inspired by Iran's Islamic revolution and overthrow Iraq's secular Sunni regime. The costly eight-year war that Saddam started between Iran and Iraq resulted in millions of casualties and great property damage to both countries. Iraq's new post-Saddam government issued a formal apology for the war and other crimes committed against Iran by Saddam's regime. The head of **SCIRI (Supreme Council for Islamic Revolution in Iraq), Abdel Aziz al-Hakim,** also advocated paying Iran billions of dollars in reparations for damage resulting from the Iran-Iraq war.

---

[157]More than 60% of Iraq's population is Shi'ite Muslim.

2003 Operation Iraqi Freedom

Relations between Iran and Iraq changed drastically after the U.S. invasion of Iraq in 2003 and Saddam Hussein's fall from power.

Without the war, Saddam Hussein would have been free to continue developing weapons of mass destruction (WMD) which would likely have been used against Iran as they had in the past.[158]

The fall of Saddam also led to the rise of Iraq's religious Shi'ites who came to power in the first open and free election the country had seen in decades.

With the U.S. bogged down in Iraq, focus shifted away from America's grievances with Iran. And with America's sullied reputation over intelligence blunders and flawed claims about the progress of Iraq's nuclear weapons program, the U.S. government has been careful not to make grand allegations about Iran's own nuclear program.

Political Alliances

Many Iraqi Shi'a clerics were forced to flee to Iran under threat of death or imprisonment during the dark days of Saddam Hussein's brutal secular reign. When Ayatollah Khomeini came to power, he suggested that the Iraqi expatriates form an umbrella organization, the **Supreme Council for Islamic Revolution (SCIRI),** which would eventually take over Iraq. Since its inception in 1980, SCIRI received military training, political support and financing from Iran's government while it engaged in political activity against Saddam Hussein's regime. SCIRI's leader, **Ayatollah Sayed Mohammed Baqir al-Hakim** returned to Iraq in 2003 with SCIRI's military arm, the **Badr Brigade,** in order to participate in the new post-Saddam Iraqi government.

When Hakim was killed in a car bomb in August 2003, his brother, Syed Abdul Aziz al-Hakim took over as leader and served as President of the Interim Iraqi Governing Council when it convened in December the same year.

In January 2005, SCIRI joined the **United Iraqi Alliance** which won 41% of Iraqi votes in the December 15, 2005 general election giving it 128 of the 275 seats in Iraq's parliament.

---

[158] Chemical and biological weapons were employed against Iranians a number of times between 1983 and 1986 to deflect the human-wave attacks. By 1986, it is estimated that Iraqi chemical warfare was responsible for about 10,000 casualties. In 1988, Iraq integrated nerve agent strikes into its offensive, leading to a cease-fire between the two nations.

SANCTIONS

The United States was Iran's biggest trading partner before the 1979 revolution, buying more than 20% of Iran's imports. But economic relations between the two countries rapidly deteriorated after the revolution due to the new regime's anti-American rhetoric and the ensuing 444-day hostage crisis. In order to try to coerce Iran into releasing the Americans held in the U.S. Embassy, then-U.S. President Jimmy Carter enacted the first in a series of formal sanctions blocking trade between the two countries.

Most of the initial trade restrictions were dropped once the hostages were released in 1981. But Iran's participation in the bombing of the U.S. Embassy and Marine barracks in Lebanon and the country's subsequent designation as a "sponsor of international terrorism" compelled Carter's successor, President Ronald Reagan, to renew sanctions in the mid 1980s. Trade restrictions were broadened in the late 1980s in retaliation for Iran's attack on neutral oil tankers in the Persian Gulf during the 1980-1988 Iran-Iraq war. They were expanded again in the early 1990s as part of U.S. President Bill Clinton's "dual containment" plan to prevent both Iran and Iraq from making trouble in the Middle East by keeping them economically weak.

After a string of terrorist attacks on Israelis by Iranian-supported organizations (HAMAS, Palestinian Islamic Jihad and others), the United States decided to implement its farthest reaching trade embargo to date by enacting the **Iran-Libya Investment Sanctions (ILSA)** which threatened non-American firms with economic penalties if they invested more than $20 million in Iran's oil industry. It was reasoned that by curtailing profits earned from oil exports (which accounted for more than 80% of Iran's income), Iran would be less able to fund international terrorism or develop weapons of mass destruction (WMD). U.S. President George W. Bush renewed ILSA in August 2001 for five more years.

As long as Iran continues to develop its nuclear program, support terrorists, oppose the Middle East Peace movement and deem America its enemy, the United States will likely maintain its trade embargo.

BACKGROUND

Before the 1979 Islamic Revolution, Iran was one of America's closest allies and the U.S. was Iran's number one trade partner.

Diplomatic and economic relations between the two countries were damaged when a mob of Iranian students besieged the American Embassy and held 60 of the occupants hostage.

In response, U.S. President Jimmy Carter applied economic pressure on Iran: first by imposing a ban on the import of Iranian oil to the U.S., by freezing billions of dollars worth of Iranian assets[159] and finally by instituting an embar-

---

[159] By "freezing Iran's assets" the U.S. government prohibited Iranians from transferring or pulling money out of bank accounts in the United States. The freeze was carried out in response to rumor that Iran intended to remove all of its dollar deposits from U.S. banks (which would have gravely affected the American economy).

go on U.S. exports to Iran. Carter also prohibited Americans from traveling to Iran or conducting any financial transactions in the country.[160]

With the loss of its biggest trading partner, Iran was forced to form new economic relationships with other countries. Since it was believed that the United States would hinder trade between Iran and Japan or Western Europe (both powerful U.S. allies), the Iranians decided to conduct trade with smaller Eastern European countries, Islamic countries and non-aligned nations.

Most of the trade restrictions were dropped when the hostages were finally released in January 1981, and a large portion of the Iranian assets that had been frozen in U.S. banks were returned to Iran.

Lebanon and the Iran-Iraq War
Following the Israeli invasion of Lebanon in 1982, Iran helped organize, finance and train a group of Lebanese Shi'a's through the creation of **Hezbollah**. In 1983, the organization was found responsible for bombing the U.S. Embassy and Marine barracks in Lebanon. As a result, Iran was declared a "sponsor of international terrorism."

Because of Iran's new status as a terrorist state and its ongoing war with Iraq, the United States decided to curtail and then ban the sale of arms, aircraft, helicopters and other military items to the country and deemed Iran ineligible to receive various forms of U.S. foreign assistance.

Economic relations between Iran and the United States worsened in the late 1980s when Iran began attacking neutral oil-shipping tankers in the Persian Gulf in the course of the Iran-Iraq War (a phase of the battle that was labeled the "Tanker War"). In October 1987, U.S. President Ronald Reagan enacted **Executive Order 12613** forbidding the importation of Iranian goods or services into the United States.

To compensate for the ban on military sales from the U.S., Iran formed an economic and military alliance with **Russia**. From 1989 on, Russia became Iran's primary supplier of combat aircraft and diesel powered submarines for the Iranian navy. Russia also began to negotiate the reconstruction of the nuclear power reactor in **Bushehr**, Iran, and the two countries agreed to cooperate on the exploration and extraction of oil from the Caspian Sea.

Post Iran-Iraq War
After eight years of war with Iraq (and repeated attacks on the both countries' oil fields), Iran's oil industry was beleaguered. For Iran, which relied on oil for 95% of its income from exports, the loss of oil production and the drop in crude oil prices in 1986, had forced Iran to concentrate on rebuilding its production capabilities, developing non-oil export products[161] and fostering more open foreign trade.

---

[160] At the time, the U.S. administration was planning a rescue mission and wanted to be sure that there were no Americans in the country who could be used as pawns of an Iranian reprisal.

[161] In 1979, oil and gas accounted for 95% of all of Iran's exports. Its second source of export revenue, carpets, only made up 1.8% of Iran's export trade. By the mid 1990s, oil was only responsibly for 82% of the country's export income and carpets accounted for 6.6% of export trade.

United States trade sanctions were also relaxed during this period.

In a short time, American oil companies once again became Iran's primary buyers of crude oil (most shipped to U.S. subsidiaries in Europe) and European countries were more openly conducting business with Iran.

Changes in the 1990s

In the early 1990s a number of events took place within the United States and internationally that affected Iranian-American relations politically and economically. In 1990, Iraqi President Saddam Hussein decided to attack Kuwait. Among other reasons, he wanted to get the country to forgive Iraq's debts from the Iran-Iraq war.

A year later, the Soviet Union collapsed releasing a number of former republics from membership in the Soviet Empire and leaving the United States as the sole global superpower. The fall of America's former Cold War nemesis allowed the U.S. to redesign its foreign policy (which was once devoted to curbing the spread of Soviet communism) in order to focus on other foreign threats – especially those emanating from the Middle East.

In less than a month, the United States (backed by a 38-member coalition of nations) expelled Iraqi forces from Kuwait, imposed economic sanctions and set up no-fly zones within Iraq to protect the Shi'as in the south and the Kurds in the north from air attacks. A U.N.-sponsored multinational security regime was then put in place while inspectors combed the country for nuclear weapons and other weapons of mass destruction (WMDs).

With the Iraqis under close guard and weakened by sanctions, the administration of President **George H. Bush** revisited the advancement of peace between Israel and its Arab neighbors — believed to be the root cause of turmoil in the Middle East. But to keep the Israelis at the bargaining table, the U.S. government had to demonstrate that it was taking measures to prevent attacks from Iraq (which had fired missiles at Israeli cities during the 1991 Gulf War) and Iran (which had stepped up support for anti-Israeli terrorist groups during the peace movement).

To keep both countries in check, Bush's successor, **Bill Clinton**, drew up a "**dual containment**" strategy. The plan was designed to strain the economic development of Iraq and Iran to stop them from funding terrorism, subverting neighboring governments, developing weapons of mass destruction or taking the region by force. Since Iraq was already immobilized, the United States applied a series of trade measures to keep Iran in an equally weakened state and tried to persuade Japan, Europe, China and Russia to limit their involvement with Iran.

To get around the sanctions, Iran strengthened its regional partnerships with countries to the east (India and Pakistan) and the former Soviet Republics of Kazakhstan and Turkmenistan. Iran also lured Western companies into investing in its oil industry by offering lucrative contracts.

Contrary to the objectives set forth in the "dual containment" plan, by 1995 American oil companies had become the primary buyers of Iran's crude oil, the U.S. had become one of the largest buyers of Iranian exports and the American firm, **Conoco,** was offered a contract worth more than $600 million by the **National Iranian Oil Company** (NIOC) to develop two offshore oil and gas fields in the Persian Gulf – all at a time when the U.S. was trying to persuade its allies to stop dealing with Iran.

In Israel, meanwhile, terrorists from the Palestinian groups **HAMAS** and **Islamic Jihad** (PIJ) (both known to have been receiving financial assistance from Iran) stepped up bombing attacks against Israeli citizens hoping to undermine the peace movement.[162]

Iran's support for terrorist activity was compounded by the announcement that Iran had signed a deal with Russia to complete construction on nuclear power reactors in **Bushehr.** Israel had also claimed that Iran was acquiring components that could be used to build nuclear weapons.

Israeli concerns were articulated in Washington D.C. by Jewish lobbyists from the **American Israel Public Affairs Committee (AIPAC)** who argued that the **Dual Containment** plan wasn't putting much pressure on Iran at all – especially considering that Americans had become Iran's third largest trading partner. Instead, AIPAC lobbyists called for a total U.S. trade embargo and boycotts against foreign companies that traded with Iran.

ILSA (Iran-Libya Investment Sanctions, 1996 to present)
In response to Iran's menacing activity and pressure within the U.S. government, the Clinton administration issued **Executive Order 12957** in March 1995 prohibiting American companies[163] from conducting any kind of trade with Iran. In May, **Executive Order 12959** was issued, imposing a total trade and investment embargo.[164]

The new sanctions did hurt the Iranians to some degree until they found new buyers for their oil at the same price.

Just a year after the Executive Orders were delivered, though, 59 Israelis were killed in 4 suicide attacks launched by HAMAS and PIJ (costing Shimon Peres the election), and a truck bomb exploded at the Khobar Towers housing complex inhabited by American military personnel killing 19 Americans and wounding another 372 people.

In frustration, the U.S. government imposed the most far-reaching sanction to date, the **Iran-Libya**[165] **Sanctions Act of 1996 (ILSA)** restricting non-U.S. firms from investing in Iran's oil sector. According to the terms of the bill,

---

[162] Terrorist attacks accelerated in 1995 and 1996 in order to subvert the reelection of Israeli Prime Minister Shimon Peres, an advocate for peace in the Middle East. As anticipated, Israeli voters instead elected hard-liner Benjamin Netanyahu.

[163] **Conoco** was forced to turn down the $600 million contract with Iran after the deal was deemed inconsistent with U.S. policy.

[164] Sanctions were temporarily waived in 2003 to allow aid into the Iranian city of Bam after a devastating earthquake.

[165] Libya had been added to the bill in response to Libya's bombing of Pan Am flight 103 over Scotland.

non-U.S. companies who invested more than $20 million in one year in Iran's oil industry would be subject to a series of sanctions placed against them by the U.S. government. The purpose was to deny Iran the hard currency it needed to buy weapons, nuclear materials and fund terrorist operations.

The Act was greatly criticized by Europeans who felt the bill violated principles of free trade and amounted to economic warfare against America's allies. **ILSA** was particularly damaging to countries such as Germany, France and Japan, who had loaned Iran billions of dollars following the Iran-Iraq war and relied on trade with Iran to recover the debts.

In retaliation, the **European Union** (EU) adopted "blocking legislations" that threatened to impose sanctions on companies that appeared to be *complying* with **ILSA**. Some companies simply ignored the sanctions (the French company **Total**, for example signed the $600 million contract that Conoco was forced to turn down) and others went around the sanctions by using oil swap deals rather than purchasing oil directly from Iran.

Nevertheless, George W. Bush renewed ILSA in August, 2001 – a month before the terrorist attacks on New York City.

Years after the passage of ILSA, Iran was still considered a state sponsor of terrorism earning the country the designation as a member of George Bush's so-called "Axis of Evil." Analysts have pointed to the weak application of penalties against countries that violate ILSA (in certain cases, the U.S. government can and has granted waivers to selected companies that do business in Iran) as a cause.

The sanctions have also prevented American firms from bidding on lucrative contracts in Iran to the benefit of European and Asian companies. China, India, Russia and Japan have taken over where America and Europe left off. China, which needs Iran's energy resources has become a big importer of Iranian oil, India and Iran have been working on a deal to construct an oil pipeline connecting the two countries, Russia has been building a billion dollar nuclear reactor in Bushehr, and 20% of Iran's exports are sold to Japan.

U.S. sanctions have also forced Iran to become more self-sufficient and reduce the country's dependence on oil for its export revenues.

On the other hand, just the threat of being excluded from the American market has discouraged many non-U.S. companies from taking any chances by investing in a country that is a financial gamble anyway. To compensate for the risk, Iran must offer higher returns for companies that do choose to invest in Iran.

In the long run, sanctions have also effectively limited Iran's access to Western technology, hard currency, Western supplies and financing, all of which contribute to Iran's economic hardship.

If Iran is found to have violated the terms of the Nuclear Non-Proliferation Treaty, the country may face even greater, multinational sanctions imposed by the United Nations Security Council.

Other books by Amanda Roraback

Afghanistan in a Nutshell
Iraq in a Nutshell
Pakistan in a Nutshell
Israel-Palestine in a Nutshell
Islam in a Nutshell

Please look for future Nutshell Notes:
"Korea in a Nutshell," "China in a Nutshell," "Mexico in a Nutshell"

Bibliography

The information contained herein is of general historical knowledge and can be supported by any Western encyclopedia, historical or geographical source books. The writer has used accredited newspaper and library sources for contemporary events that are considered factual.

The purpose of this series is not to emphasize contradictory information but to take a central point of view. The author has made all attempts to maintain a neutral position and to make this book as accurate as possible.

Extensive research has been done using well-cited secondary sources, personal interviews, newspapers and other media. A partial bibliographer is available on the Enisen website, www.enisen.com.

For more information about Enisen Publishing and for additional information about Iran, please visit www.enisen.com.